FROM TRAUMA TO TREPIDATION

Memories Transmitted by
Hidden Children to the Second Generation

by Ingrid Kisliuk

NANOMIR PRESS

NEWTON, MASSACHUSETTS

ISBN: 0-9663440-1-4

Published by Nanomir Press, 2008
Newton, Massachusetts, Unites States of America

Production & Design: Robert B. Smyth
Cover photo: George Brawerman
BackCover Photo: Susan Wilson
Logo By: Viviana Levinson

Inquiries should be addressed to:
Nanomir Press, P. O. Box 600577, Newton, MA 02460-0005

Library of Congress Catalog Number: 2008903864
Kisliuk, Ingrid
FROM TRAUMA TO TREPIDATION
Memories Transmitted by Hidden Children to the Second Generation
Printed in the United States Of America

To Roy, my husband

Contents

PREFACE

The writing of this book was prompted by the contribution of my two daughters in the Afterword of my memoir, *Unveiled Shadows*.[1] Reading their remarks enlightened me concerning their behavior during their adolescence and teenage years. Their accounts of their experience and feelings showed me that the voice of the Second Generation, that of the children of hidden children, needed to be heard. Testimonies of children of death camp survivors have been told,[2] yet this has generally not been the case for the offspring of hidden children. Although some writings that deal with the testimonies of children of camp survivors have included some children of hidden children, for the most part the effects of the trauma experienced by this category of child survivor of the Holocaust, as transmitted to their children, still needs to be documented.

I have included here my daughters' commentaries regarding life growing up as children of a hidden child, given that the present writing deals with this very subject. Their discussions follow hereafter and precede the testimonies of my interviewees.

---

1 Unveiled Shadows - The Witness of a Child, Nanomir Press, 1998, Newton, Massachusetts.
2 For example see: Children of the Holocaust, Penguin Books, 1988, New York, NY

Commentary by
CLAUDETTE BEIT-AHARON

My mother's book is a gift for all our family so that we can remember and mourn the loss of all those people we never had the privilege to meet, and those we knew who suffered to the end of their days with the horror of what they lost.

My Grandmother Helene, I knew as a bitter, sad, and always profoundly disoriented person. She never mastered English enough to have a regular conversation with me. She had a beautiful singing voice, but always sang those same songs of her youth in Vienna, *Wien, Wien nur Du allein*, and others, because for her, after she left Vienna, life would never truly be sweet again, though she was to live another forty-three years. She was, even as a very old lady, extremely pretty, and looked at least ten years younger than she was.

I remember her sitting in front of the TV with my Grandfather Saly in the mid-sixties. The strong, overwhelming Florida sun was streaming through the closed white drapes of the "Florida Room" in Hollywood. They were watching a documentary about Hitler's triumphant entrance into Vienna, the crowd roaring their approval, the buildings strewn with banners. They sat through the whole program shaking their heads, saying "my, my," as if they still couldn't believe that it had really happened. I remember asking them why they were watching it, why they tortured themselves, as they knew all that would be said--they had been there! But for some reason they were riveted to the show. Maybe they wanted to be sure that the story was told correctly, and that the Austrians weren't left off the hook. I implored them to turn it off, but they couldn't. They sat there mesmerized, with tears in their eyes.

My grandfather had a much better command of English, and I remember many nice conversations with him. He told me about waiting as a young man in Munich all night with his sister Frieda (also murdered with her husband after they were deported from Nice, France) to get tickets to hear the great Caruso. He was a wonderful grandfather and I loved him dearly. He died in 1975 while I was in Israel. He has visited me in my dreams, so vivid I can smell his scent, and see his tummy jiggle when he laughs. He told me how he felt about many things in life when I was a teenager. One conversation stands out clearly in my mind. I was fourteen years old, and I was sitting with him in his little white Toyota. In the early seventies such a small car was a novelty. It was a balmy Florida evening, my parents, sister, and grandmother had gone for a stroll. I elected to stay behind with him because his legs gave him trouble and he couldn't walk very far. We talked about his life long before the war, when he had a store in Munich. He told me about his sisters and other friends, bike trips with his brother-in-law Jacques, and other high jinks of his youth. He said that it was sad for him that we didn't know German, since this English business was so hard for him and "Mama." He never referred to my grandmother by her first name. They always called each other "Mama" and "Papa."

Growing up I was always aware of my mother's insecurities, and her ambivalence about her identity from so many directions. Her attempts to appear totally American or, Belgian in different circumstances. I had always known her to wear her heart on her sleeve. Yet, clearly she must have had some skills as a child in concealing her feelings, or she wouldn't have survived. I remember her being incredibly (to me, at the time) upset when I told her that what she thought of a person was written all over her face, or that a friend found her accent charming. She strove to have no accent.

I always thought that given her background, she coped pretty well. But I understood that there were triggers to be avoided, and I avoided them. Somehow I knew that they were not about me at all, and that the source was something I couldn't understand. Her growth through writing these memoirs has been truly amazing.

Though the journey was difficult and painful, the results have been constructive. It is sad that my grandparents couldn't live to be part of the healing--forty years was not enough time.

My grandparents never talked about their daughter Herta. I believe that they could no longer bring themselves to tell her story, it was too painful for them. They would just point out her picture and sigh. My grandmother especially was very untrusting of the intentions of the world at large. She had a hard time letting us out of her sight when we visited them in Florida. She had good reason to feel that way, and to be obsessed about abductions. We laughed off her seriousness at the threats that she perceived everywhere, which must have been especially frustrating for her.

Growing up, I knew somehow that my mother didn't feel that she had definite proof that her sister Herta had died. When I went to Israel in 1974 at eighteen, I felt that I should be looking for Herta. Perhaps she had survived. I searched the faces on the bus in Haifa, those broken people with the tattooed numbers on their arms, for traces of the pretty young woman whose face had always occupied a central spot in my grandparents' home. I tried to force myself to go to the Yad Vashem memorial, research center, and museum to try to look her name up--but somehow the thought was paralyzing. I dreamed of a reunion. . . . My poor Grandpa died at about that time. But still I half-looked for her in every public place.

This background instilled in me caution so that I am never comfortable unless I have a valid passport, and I always know that it is close by.

I am fair skinned and have blue eyes. As a little girl I had blond hair. That pleased my mother no end. She always admired northern European coloring, finding it more attractive than dark-ones. I remember one day when I was thirteen, I came downstairs with my hair in two braids by my ears. She laughed and said "I could have named you Gretchen." She was not indicating that this would have been a good idea, but was clearly pleased that I could have "passed" if I had to.

She had picked our names because of her love of French, but I think that our names were also part of her continuing hiding, and she just wanted us to be safe. But it was really ironic, for here I was, proud to identify as a Jew, and Jews were constantly questioning my origins because of a non-Jewish appearance, and my first name.

My mother, out of necessity, had hidden her Jewish identity, and one of the results was that she heard lots of anti-Semitic remarks that she might not have heard otherwise by so-called friends. I was not interested in hiding at all, and yet I also heard many an anti-Semitic remark. Unless I made an announcement, bigots had no idea that one of "them" was hearing these statements. In order to protect myself from hearing these epithets, I always found a way to announce my ethnicity as soon as possible in social situations.

My Jewish identity and that of my children is supremely important to me. I pray and hope that they will sanctify the memories of our dear families, and all the extended family of the murdered Jewish People, by living strong lives of Jewish commitment. As I watched my mother's struggles with her insecurities, I decided that the only way that I could do something about what happened before I was born was by living as positive a Jewish life as I could, and raising my children the same way.

Of course, none of this would have been possible if my mother had not been that defiant little girl in the convent school, resisting the brainwashing, brushing off the signs of the cross, and staying true to who she was.

Commentary by
MICHELLE KISLIUK

In 1991, while I was a graduate student in New York City, by chance in an office waiting room somewhere, I came across a glossy spread in New York Magazine describing the upcoming First International Gathering of Children Hidden During World War II. I had never really understood my mother's reluctance to speak about, or really address her past. I sent her that article, thinking that maybe this event might provide a new context for tracing that painful time.

As a child, I had always interpreted my mother's reluctance to speak of that time, and her apparent bitterness about it, as my being unworthy of hearing about such important things. Now, reading *Unveiled Shadows* I wonder if this feeling was passed on to me--the youngest in the family--in a way that mirrored how my mother was treated by the adults around her during her own childhood. In order to protect her, they did not explain things to her, which left her feeling lonely, guilty, and confused. My mother, too, wanted to protect me. Unlike my sister, who says that she somehow always knew that my mother's feelings had nothing to do with her, I internalized or inherited a deep sense of guilt, sure that I was to blame for my mother's bitterness, convinced that were I different, I could have prevented her feeling that way. Something was hidden--something very bad that we could never change.

The feeling in me began as guilt, and grew into anger and frustration during my adolescence, but with no way yet to pinpoint the roots of these feelings. Becoming an adult has for me, among other things, been a process of coming to understand the circumstances of my family history. Now, especially, with the help of my mother's book, I begin to see that my mother's efforts to protect me from hurt she had suffered were, on one level, in vain; experience gets passed on, if not directly, then indirectly. The chance to heal from the pain of that time comes only with the direct confrontation with the past that *Unveiled Shadows* offers.

Four years younger than my sister, as a child I knew my grandparents only as old people. Like my sister, I too was especially fond of my Grandpa and remember vividly how it felt to sit on his lap: holding his strong, kind hands, his jokes, his little songs as he bounced me on his knee, "I love you, a bushel and a peck, a bushel and a peck, and a hug around the neck." Somehow, because of his accent, I thought of these as German or Yiddish songs, like *"By mir bist du shein,"* when in reality these were all American ditties popular in the forties and fifties. I did know my grandfather well enough that now, when I read about that terrible time when he said, sobbing, *"Mein bestes Kind haben sie mir genommen"* ("They took my best child") I am transported to the moment and hear and see vividly, and feel deeply, my little-girl mother's wretchedness, and my grandfather's pain.

Though I loved my grandmother, I found it difficult to understand her--literally, in terms of language, and more figuratively, in terms of her personality. Sometimes she frightened me with cruel jokes when I was very little. When I was a bit older, she would warn me not to go outside alone, saying "someone will shteal (steal) you . . . ." I scoffed at her idea, not knowing the roots of her fears. When she was very old, after my grandfather had died, she once warned me never to trust a non-Jew, because in reality they all want to kill us, she told me. Now that I understand, with the help of the details in my mother's book, what my poor grandmother lived through. I know what she was trying to tell me, and that she wanted to protect me. With the help of the book, I have come to know my grandparents better now, and to know my mother better too. I am also especially grateful to have a chance now to know my aunt Herta a little bit. I was robbed of my aunt - and my uncle - and the children they would have had, and I palpably feel that void.

When I was about eleven years old, I sang in a children's chorus the piece "I Never Saw Another Butterfly," based on poems by Jewish children who perished in the Nazi genocide. My grandparents attended a performance at our synagogue, and afterwards my mother told me that my grandfather had cried. Hearing this I felt at once guilty and confused. Was he just proud of me? But then why would he cry? I could not understand the extent of his feelings and associations. I tried unsuccessfully to convince myself that this reaction was only sentimentality. But with a lingering feeling of inauthenticity, I could sense that the truth must be too much for me to suddenly bear, that I was not fully enough of a person to comprehend and participate in these feelings. I think now, though, that I was enough of a person, and though it would have been hard, my mother and grandparents' confiding in me would have grounded me in a way that I needed as I moved into adolescence. But ultimately, there is no way to know, in retrospect, what might have been best.

Certain bits of the story in my mother's book I have indeed known about since I was a child. For example, I knew that my mother would wipe off the sign of the cross when she was at the convent school, and about hiding among the furs when the Nazis came. But I never heard the story so vividly as told in the book, and had never heard many aspects, such as the story about my uncle Ernst's girlfriend who bought candies for my mother --the orange peels covered with chocolate. Other stories I had never heard; for example, that for quite some time my mother called herself "Irène." I do have a faint recollection, as a small child, of thinking that my aunt Herta was lost somewhere and might be found. Then, at some point, I sensed in my mother an unexplained shift to sadness and despair.

When I visited my parents soon after they returned from the meeting in Belgium, my mother showed me the names of our murdered relatives listed in the *Mémorial de la Déportation des Juifs de Belgique*.[1] Of course, I began to cry. My mother seemed surprised that I would cry, or maybe she was afraid that this could be so close to me, emotionally, after she had gone to such efforts to keep me at a distance from all this. But the message is clear now. I appreciate her trying to protect me and my sister. Who knows what other scars we would bear had she told us all when we were small?

Nevertheless, there was ultimately no way to avoid the pain, because it came through in other ways anyway. Not understanding my mother's feelings--for example, her relationship to the French language, and her wish that her daughters learn it impeccably --inevitably affected my growing up and formed my personality. In my life and work I champion the vernacular as a place of depth, resistance, difference, legitimacy, and I generally distrust official and chauvinistic culture.

My identity as a Jew has long been important to me. My parents made every effort to provide me with a progressive Jewish education, and I was a Bat Mitzvah. But this particular history of my family has also always been with me, and my mother's book validates us. It is our history, and it fills a hole or erases a question mark in my identity that was felt, but not fully understood.

In my teaching and research I fight against racial and ethnic bigotry, and toward cross-cultural understanding. Teaching in Virginia with relatively few Jewish students, I always mention my background and my family history and make analogies to the dangers of fascist ways of thinking and being. Race and ethnic hatred is still our biggest danger in this time, both nationally and internationally. My own work, in Africa and in the United States, is integrated at all levels with my life, and is deeply about combating hatred and fostering understanding.

The seeds of my life were sown, sometimes in mysterious ways, in the experience of my parents and grandparents. I thank my mother for the enormous effort it took to write this book, and am deeply grateful to my father for loving and supporting my mother, for enabling her to give us this very precious and lasting gift.

NOTES:

1. Mémorial de la Déportation des Juifs de Belgique, by Serge Klarsfeld and Maxime Steinberg, listing the 25,257 Jews deported from Belgium who perished in Nazi death camps. The Beate Klarsfeld Foundation, 1982, New York, NY

INTRODUCTION

In considering how this writing came about, it is crucial to answer the following questions. What did hidden children pass on to the next generation, those whose parents, in order to save them, gave them away to strangers who hid them? What did these hidden children, the ones whose parents never returned from death camps, and who grew up unaware of their real identity, convey to their own children? What was transmitted by those who as children hid in monasteries, in convents, in orphanages, on farms; who were often on the run because collaborators denounced their hiding places to the Nazis? In some situations the lucky ones survived with their parents, or at least with one parent, or with some other relative. However, in every instance, hidden children had no childhood; it was stolen from them. Many of these children, having had no parental role model, were later unsuccessful as parents themselves. This was often the case when both partners grew up in orphanages. And though some may have faltered as parents, a great number of these hidden children still became successful professionals as adults.

Who, then, *are* the offspring of these traumatized children? Sometimes they are the children of orphans whose sons and daughters urge their parents to search for their family's history. The children are avid to learn their family's story and often they are desolated by their parents' avoidance of the subject or their total silence in some instances.

In the fall of 1999 and the spring and summer of 2000, I collected testimonies from children of hidden children living in the United States, Israel, Belgium, and France. I also interviewed one

1

person in Prague, in 1999, when I attended a gathering of child survivors of the holocaust in that city. The ages of these women and men ranged from twenty-two to mid-forties. They were the children of child survivors who, between the ages of three and thirteen, escaped being sent to death camps because they were hidden. I taped all interviews except for two, and selected fourteen to include here, out of a total of ninety-eight. I chose some from each country. Many of the witnesses I interviewed were pleasantly surprised to find that they belonged to a special group whose experience they shared. They expressed gratitude that their lives were being considered, and were recognized as valuable.

Murray, an architect from New York in his mid-forties, put it very concisely in an email message to me after our meeting. His mother was hidden in Athens with a Greek Christian family, his mother's younger sister and his grandparents, along with other members of his family, were deported to death camps from Salonika, Greece. None of them ever returned. Of the seventy seven thousand Jews who lived in Greece before World War II, only about six thousand survived. Murray wrote:

> *I had never thought of myself as part of a group. In all honesty, I am surprised at how upsetting our interview was for me although I couldn't be happier that you are pursuing this project and that I could be included. It's obviously gratifying when someone is interested in a subject, which cuts to the heart of who one is.*

Some of the interviewees didn't want their names mentioned; others didn't mind.

Since several people preferred to stay anonymous, I decided to use fictitious names for all the testifiers except for an occasional first name. I asked everyone the same questions, allowing them to speak freely, and breaking in only to ask for clarification. The interviews generally spanned two to three hours; but sometimes lasted longer. On several occasions, our meetings resulted in an enriched relationship between the children and their hidden children parents.

In the United States I conducted interviews in the Greater Boston area; in the New York City area, including New Jersey; in the Washington, D.C. area, and in Baltimore, Md. The Hidden Child Foundation in New York City helped me in my search for witnesses. Their office sent out a mailing describing my project to the children of hidden children on their list, which occasioned some direct contacts from them to me. Other children of hidden children came forth when the message was transmitted by word of mouth through family, friends, and acquaintances. One witness withdrew from testifying because her mother objected to her participation.

In early September of 1999, I attended a conference of Child Survivors of the Holocaust in Prague, as mentioned above. This was the first gathering of its kind to take place in a former Communist country. I had the privilege of reaching some people of the second generation. However, none were of the local community, mainly because the Czech Jewish Community's organizers lacked the experience with this kind of gathering. They were not prepared to facilitate my meeting with the local children of hidden children.

At our hotel, I met Debra, an engaging young American woman, then living in Los Angeles. I found her reasoning edifying concerning some aspects of the Conference, which engendered disturbing effects in the second generation attendees. Her testimony explaining her viewpoints is featured further in this book.

After the conference in the Czech Republic, I made my way to Brussels, Belgium, the city where I grew up and where I was a hidden child during the German occupation of that country during World War II. While there I was invited to a meeting of a group of fourteen people who were children of hidden children. This occurred due to the careful ministration of Myriam, one of the group members, who is also my friend Ilse's daughter.

My childhood friend Ilse and I reconnected through the strangest coincidence. I had lost track of Ilse for many decades, we had known each other as little girls in Brussels, she was two years my senior. Then in 1995, at a gathering in Brussels of persons hidden as children in Belgium during World War II, I encountered by chance a mutual childhood friend, Edith, now living in Israel. More than seven hundred people attended the conference, and that afternoon the large amphitheatre was filled. My husband and I mounted the steps to an upper row where we spotted two seats available next to the isle seat already taken. I apologized for troubling the woman who stood up to let us through. As I weaved past her and turned to sit down, she excitedly grabbed me and kissed me, calling all the while, over and over, "Inge Scheer, Inge Scheer." I was dumbfounded to hear this name that I had not been called since childhood. It was my maiden name combined with my former first name. I had long disliked and rejected it, for besides the pain that it recalled, no Belgian had been able to pronounce "Inge" properly, and it had made me stand out immediately as a foreigner. I had discarded this name in 1942 when, going into hiding, I sought to blend in with the local population, and at that time I changed it to Irène. Hearing someone call me Inge brought forth deep discomfort because that name symbolized for me years of profound unhappiness. Now, all of a sudden it seemed to emerge from some distant depth, ringing totally alien in the ears of my evolved persona five decades later. Bewildered, we stared at each other. She spoke her own former name: Edith Berger! For the moment, it meant nothing to me. I recognized neither her face nor her name. How could she know me, how could she recognize me? Then she reminded me that her sister Mathilde had been my classmate. Together we had played hopscotch and jump rope. After going into hiding, we had all lost track of each other. Suddenly, fifty-three years later, here we were again, meeting by mere chance. I was stunned. Knowing that most of my Jewish playmates and classmates had been deported and killed, I never expected to see anyone I had known as a child.

Sometime later at a different occasion, Edith, who also knew Ilse since childhood found her and told her about me, after which Ilse and I started corresponding. I had already known that she had survived the Nazi occupation by hiding in a convent. But I also knew that she had stayed there even after the allied armies liberated Brussels in September 1944. Both of Ilse's parents perished after the Nazis deported them to death camps. At the time, some of my parents' acquaintances who knew Ilse well speculated that she would become a nun. But later I heard that she left the convent, married, and had three children. She still lives in Belgium, as do her two sons and her daughter. Her husband, who was sixteen years her senior, had already passed away by the time we reconnected. Knowing about my work concerning hidden children's transmission of their experiences to the next generation, Ilse informed me of her own children's interest. Her daughter, who is the oldest, and her middle son are both absorbed with the subject.

Shortly after we started corresponding, Ilse telephoned my home in the Boston area from Belgium, telling me that she and her daughter would be coming to New Jersey to attend a wedding. This was to be her first trip to the United States. Hence, I became reacquainted again with my childhood friend whom I hadn't seen in fifty-four years. We had last glimpsed one another shortly after the war, in 1945, when my mother and I sat in window seats in a streetcar. At a stop in the heart of Brussels, we heard a knocking at the side of the car by someone below in the street. There was Ilse, who was then about fifteen years old, beaming and waving, accompanied by a smiling young nun. As the streetcar started to move, my mother and I excitedly waved back to Ilse, who kept walking along the moving streetcar, still beaming and waving. She found out at that moment that I, too, had survived. More than half a century later, she related the incident to me in a letter; I remembered.

Our meeting in New Jersey was joyous. It was a miracle that we found each other again. I also met her daughter Myriam, mentioned above, who was interested in participating in this study. During our interview, Myriam informed me that in Brussels she belonged to a group of children of hidden children who met monthly to lend support to one another and discuss the problems of transmission. This was the group of fourteen people I later met in Brussels. The people I interviewed there were distinct from the other witnesses I interviewed for this book in terms of being aware that, as children of hidden children, they belonged to a special community. Their group was an outgrowth of that first gathering in Brussels in 1995 of former hidden children. Some members of the second generation also participated in that gathering, which afforded those in Myriam's group an opportunity to meet, and form their own interest group.

Since I planned to be in Belgium after visiting Prague that coming September, Myriam offered to bring up the matter of my visit and my project with her group. The plan was to see whether group members would be willing to meet with me, as well as invite me to attend their meeting.

The members agreed; I was invited, and I also made arrangements to meet everyone separately. An invitation was also extended to my husband, who traveled with me, ever supportive of my work.

It was a glorious September in Brussels. We stayed in an Apart-hotel located in an area named Ixelles, on a side street off the lovely Avenue Louise. We hadn't realized that our lodgings were so close to 453 Avenue Louise, where during the German occupation the Nazis had housed their Gestapo headquarters. Jews, who were caught by the Nazis when they raided the streets, or a particular neighborhood, were held in the basement of that building. From there the Nazis sent them to the town of Malines, to an assembly camp about thirty kilometers from Brussels. This was the antechamber of death. When the Nazis had caught enough victims for a convoy, they expedited them to the death camps of Eastern Europe, mostly to Auschwitz, Poland. The plaque on the building at 453 Avenue Louise reads as follows, translated from the French:

> *In broad daylight, on January 20, 1943, these premises, den of the Gestapo during the War of 1940--1945, came under the avenging gunfire from the plane of Captain Baron Jean-Michel de Selys Longchamps of the 1st Regiment de Guides, flying officer of the Royal Air Force.*

A bit farther down the avenue stands a monument to the memory of this valiant Belgian captain de Selys Longchamps His Hawker Typhoon fighter swooped low over the Avenue

Louise, and then flew straight at the Gestapo Headquarters, firing a stream of deadly 20 mm. cannon fire right into their murderous headquarters which sustained substantial damage, and a number of the Nazis within were killed.[1] I remember hearing this information as a child and learning how all of Brussels was cheered by the news. We also found out that the brave pilot was able to escape and return to Great Britain with his plane.

We passed by that building on many occasions during our stay that month of September. Each time I shuddered at the thought of what happened to the people who were imprisoned there. This was the place where some of my loved ones were held, my sister, aunt, and cousins. None of them returned.

The group of children of hidden children gathered in a house on the campus of the *Université Libre de Bruxelles*. At the time, they had been meeting for over a year and a half and were ready to accept the presence of an interested visitor. People were friendly and appeared at ease with my presence. Once more I was shown gratitude for my attention; many were pleased that I was seriously interested in what they had to say. The group expressed appreciation that their experience would be substantiated in the writing of a book, that was the main reason why they accepted my presence. In addition, I had come from America, a local person would not have been invited. Although I had grown up in the same country as they had, I was *l'Américaine*.

The meeting started at 8:30 pm with six people. Others joined little by little, until one hour later fourteen members were present. As was the custom, there was neither an agenda, nor was there a prearranged topic to be discussed.

Seated around a large table, people socialized and chatted, which was the accustomed way their meetings began. I was informed that it could take a couple of hours before the discussion would take off, when, out of the general conversation, a topic would emerge. By 10 pm I took the liberty, of suggesting, that we start the discussion.

Somehow the theme of hiding, or, of revealing, the fact of coming to a meeting of children of hidden children, came to the fore.

Who did or did not acknowledge it openly? Who spoke about it to friends, or put it prominently in their calendar? And if not, why not?

Also, we spoke about the matter of passing *le flambeau* (the torch,) as expressed by their parents' generation. The concern was about passing on the memory of what happened during the Holocaust to be preserved throughout the following generations. Some of the group members found it to be an imposition; they rebelled against it by mocking the endeavor. Most everyone spoke of deep personal feelings, but tried to keep the debate on an upbeat tone, often making light of their personal pain. Some spoke of what had befallen their grandparents. I was shaken when one man in his mid-forties, his voice trembling with outrage and bitterness, recounted a conversation with a business employee who inquired about deceased members of his family:

> *What an answer I had to give! I said to her, "My grand-*
> *mother was gassed." Then he added, "Can you imagine?*
> *What a horrific and at the same time sardonic explanation!"*

The discussion was animated; I listened intently and sometimes ventured a question. By 1:30 am I excused myself. I had a 9 am appointment the following morning and a full day's work ahead of me. Besides, the debate had run its course.

I selected four testimonies from this group of fourteen witnesses. Their interviews follow in the ensuing chapters.

The following spring my husband and I traveled to Israel and France in order to meet with other children of hidden children who had grown up in those countries. I made contact with relatives and friends of witnesses whom I had met in the United States, who had suggested I seek the participation of these particular people. In Israel I was fortunate to have the assistance of Michal, my son-in-law's mother. She publicized the project in kibbutzim newsletters, with social service organizations, at universities, and through word of mouth. Her help occasioned the participation of a large number of people from various areas, resulting in a flurry of cross-country journeys for my husband and me.

Some interviewees came to meet me, others received me in their home in Jerusalem, Tel Aviv, the Haifa area, and at Michal's kibbutz in northern Israel. The two weeks spent in Israel enabled me to assemble twenty interviews.

France was the following leg of our journey. Several weeks before my arrival, my Parisian friend Sylvie, who was a member of the Paris-based organization, *Les Enfants Cachés*, (The Hidden Children) requested that my project be announced in their newsletter. At first the organizers were reluctant, and I had to assure them in writing that my plan was strictly a nonfiction literary work, not a scientific study. Finally, a small notice appeared and a number of people replied. When I arrived in Paris, I was invited to visit the office of *Les Enfants Cachés*, to meet a number of the volunteers who made up the staff. It was then that I received from them the several answers they obtained in reply to their announcement of my visit and work. I made contact with the authors of these letters and ended up meeting with most of them. Additional meetings were arranged through friends in the United States, and France. Upon my return to the United States, two of my Paris interviewees informed me that *Les Enfants Cachés* announced in their current newsletter that their group sponsored a gathering of members of the second generation. Many of the participants were people whom I interviewed in Paris. Later those who attended told me that they had found the gathering interesting and rewarding. Thus, members of the second generation in that city, realizing that they belonged to a special group, formed a new community.

In the United States, in Prague and Israel I interviewed in English; in Belgium and in France we communicated in French, and I translated these interviews. In general, since people spoke freely, their contribution had to be widely edited and consolidated to avoid repetition.

The participants in this project were bright, sensitive, and articulate. I was gratified by their sincerity and intelligence, and am immensely grateful for their confidence in me. It was a great pleasure to meet them. It is an exceptional privilege for me to relate their experiences.

As already noted, the commentaries above are taken from my memoir *Unveiled Shadows*, and are by my two daughters. The testimonies that follow begin with one interview in Prague, followed by interviews conducted in Belgium, Israel, and France. Most of the subsequent interviews took place in the United States. Those interviews were carried out at various times before, during, and after my travels abroad to the above-mentioned countries.

NOTES:

1. Captain Baron Jean Michel de Selys Longchamps – Pilot Royal Air Force. On August 16, 1943, when returning from a mission, he was killed on landing in Manston, England. Manston was formerly known as a Royal Air Force Airfield it is now the Kent International Airport.

DEBRA

MOST OF THE TIME
I DISMISS THE DISCOMFORT I FEEL DEEP DOWN,
AND CONDUCT MYSELF LIKE A NORMAL PERSON

The four-day conference in Prague, of child survivors of the Holocaust, had just ended. Debra was twenty-four at the time of our interview, in September of 1999. A native of Philadelphia, she currently lived in Los Angeles. In college she had majored in psychology, but presently she taught elementary school.

Before coming to Prague, Debra had accompanied her mother and several other participants in the conference on a trip to a number of concentration camps in Poland, including Auschwitz.

We stayed at the same hotel and met in my room.

My mother was a hidden child in Poland. She always spoke to me about her past, but I only started asking questions when I got older, when topics came up in conversation. When I was in kindergarten, my mother came to speak to my class; she is very good at speaking to children's groups. I remember having heard certain stories she told already, but I didn't dare ask again, especially after age five.

I was never rebellious as a teenager. I have always been concerned with death, and cautious to a paranoid extent. I never did anything I felt could be risky, always aware that people might die. I suspected that the world wasn't going to continue. From my mother, I gathered that not only possessions could be taken away, but life itself.

At the conference, I attended workshops for the second generation. Some people there expressed the notion that they had tried to be the perfect child in order to make up for their parents' losses. There were others who had rebelled against this compulsion to be perfect. My attitude was similar to that of the former group. I always avoided getting angry, afraid that if I did, I risked being shut out, or turned away. Often I felt guilty about not being hungry, and when I was, I felt I had no right to complain. Now, as an adult, I recognize the problem; I understand that suffering cannot be put on a scale. I was dismayed and uneasy to hear how some survivors have a hierarchy in suffering, and how they apply it to each other. In one of the workshops, a survivor compared her own suffering to the speaker's. She indicated that since she herself had suffered more, she should have been the one to speak; she had lost both parents whereas the speaker had lost only one.

Some people are so deep in their pain that they don't know how a normal person acts. The facilitator of the workshop complimented me on my apparent wholesomeness: "Look how healthy you are," she said. She attributed my apparent health to the fact that my mother hadn't hidden her past from me. I was pained by the facilitator's comments and thought them simplistic. How could this woman know, having spoken to me only for a few minutes, whether or not I am a functional person? In fact, most of the time I dismiss the discomfort I feel deep down, and conduct myself like a healthy individual. Therefore, everyone assumes that I am well, which I don't necessarily feel at all. I go through the motions successfully, but I hide deep fears. Just because a person holds down a job and functions, doesn't necessarily indicate wholesomeness.

I still don't know certain facts about my mother's experience when she was a hidden child. This is mainly due to the fact that her memory of many events is fragmented, and not necessarily chronological. Neither she nor I have attempted to make a time-line, which would clarify things for us both.

When I was in the sixth grade, we had to create a book that was based on someone's true-life story. That was when my mother told me how the mistress of a Gestapo man hid the family all around the Warsaw area. She also described how, as a child, she had to hide under a table for many days at a time. The woman who hid my mother in her home was the sister of an alcoholic Gestapo man who lived with her. He would come home, sit down at the table which was covered by a long table cloth, and often the child underneath would endure the man's kicks, but in his drunken state he never noticed. Hiding under the table had other repercussions as well, that my mother revealed to me only a short time ago. She told me that since, as a child, she was prevented from going to the toilet for so long while hiding under the table, she developed intestinal problems that are ongoing. I recounted this story for my sixth grade assignment.

I think that my mother speaks a lot more than many other people. Yet she has only mentioned to me recently certain aspects of her childhood. I knew that the worst thing that happened to her had something to do with sexuality. I have to remain vague about this aspect of my mother's experience because she had the most trouble talking about these issues. As a child I sensed that certain things that occurred were somehow bad. I wanted to protect her from being hurt, so I didn't question her further.

I also fear that my mother may feel that she was transmitting to me her own pain and trauma. In fact, she feels guilty whenever she sees me upset. She says: "I put this terrible thing on you; look what I have instilled in my children." The anguish is especially vivid since my oldest brother has been having problems; he doesn't like himself. I like myself; however, I can go through the motions, perhaps to fool others and myself. My oldest brother can't do that. I don't know what he thinks because he never says much about anything. He seems unhappy, but since he never speaks I don't know why. My middle brother appears to be do-ing well, he seems grown up, developing, and happily married. Yet this middle brother appears to be having some problems too.

I have a close relationship with his wife and she often gives me information. She speaks of what my brother is going through in terms of guilt feelings and not liking himself. My older brother is now saying, after all the unhappiness, that his children are his legacy.

Both of my brothers are much older than I. Only recently have they started to treat me as an adult. They are half brothers, children from my mother's first marriage. My brothers' father is also a hidden child, but unlike my mother, he doesn't talk. The two met during the war when my mother was hiding in a village outside Warsaw, wandering days on end with a goat. At some point she saw a train set as well as a boy. He turned out to be the same person whom she met again some years later. He became her first husband.

My father is an American Jew; he has soaked in all the anger, and has taken on the role of my mother's protector. My mother often has nightmares; she has a lot of trouble deciding with whom to be angry. She told me that, after the war, when she was about twenty years old, she would wake up the neighbors who complained about her screaming during her nightmares. So she went to a therapist who said to her words that remind me of what the workshop facilitator at the conference said to me. The therapist told my mother: "Oh, you are totally functional; you are studying, you are all grown up and going on with your life; obviously you are fine". It took my mother years before someone would actually see her. Other child survivors told me that this experience is very common among them. When I heard my mother's story about her nightmares and her screams, I tried to put myself in her place. I imagined how it would have felt, how it would have seemed, having to hide under the table all the time.

As a junior in high school, I wrote a play about the second generation. When it was produced, my brothers took turns playing my grandfather. It was the first time that the three of us discussed anything about the Holocaust. In my play, I deal with the subject of communication, especially with my grandfather, to whom I say:

"I am about to go to Poland, give me the information." But he replies: "You know nothing because it has all taken place within yourself. You don't know anything, why are you coming here? You must go and seek something else."

In the original ending of the play, the characters find some kind of connection. I won second place for my play in a contest. The person responsible for judging the work thought that there was more to be said; that if I had changed the ending I would have won first prize. My grandfather was in fact killed and shoved into a garbage can. Therefore, she recommended that at the end of the play my grandfather should be in the garbage can.

She suggested that I submit my play to a Jewish theater.

At this point Debra was overcome with emotion. She was on the verge of tears as she spoke about this episode. Controlling herself, she continued:

At first I thought: "Oh no, that's not OK," but then I realized that that was exactly what I wanted to do. In the play there is a room containing only a pile of ashes and the grandfather. When I changed the ending the protagonist ends up putting the ashes on himself and getting into the garbage can.

At the time I was a junior in high school; I didn't realize that that's what I wanted the character to do. Being so young I didn't recognize that aspect. I believe that no one wants to admit that they want to think about that kind of experience. That's what so many people want to do; because you can't . . . you don't know what it's like . . .

Debra is once more distraught, having tried to express her thoughts. We stop our discussion for her to get some tissues in the bathroom. She resumes:

The play has been produced in the theater many times. However, I feel that I ought to rewrite it. I took writing classes, but as yet I don't know what I'll do with the play.

When I joined a second-generation group, I met a young man who had also written a play, but it hadn't been chosen. He wanted to form a "Holocaust Theater." I wasn't interested, I felt that I couldn't do it; it would be too much, emotionally. The young man kept insisting; but I never went back to the group. I didn't want to be stalked by this person who was a disturbed individual. His father had been in Auschwitz and had committed suicide.

There have been conferences of child survivors almost every year for nearly ten years. This is the first one for me. I found the experience of the workshops trying. Many people I met were often just so angry. Everybody needed to get their story out, and it was clear that every one had something to contribute; but they weren't listening to each other. I wanted to hear where other people were coming from. Most second-generation children are overprotected, but one person stated that her family practically disowned her. Someone disputed this emphatically and said: "That's not what happens." I remarked to her that there were three people in the room to whom this had happened, and no one should put them down. People are making generalizations based on their own experience. I felt that there was a lack of empathy in the group.

My mother gave me the video that she made for the Shoah Foundation founded by Steven Spielberg.[1] I haven't finished watching it; I want to view it with my boyfriend and no one else. It's difficult to say "let's sit down and watch something that will make you depressed and miserable." So I have been putting it off; we'll watch it eventually.

My boyfriend's mother became a German studies major, thinking that this was a way for her to understand what had happened. My boyfriend's grandmother got out of Germany in the thirties and harbored guilt feelings. She never told his mother anything. He is now the third generation. I didn't want him to join me on this trip, and think that I deprived him and myself of an opportunity to understand and discuss how it is to grow up with people who, after they have just returned from seeing Auschwitz, attend group discussions, casually exchange observations at the dinner table, walk about and joke. I feel bad that he wasn't there, because I fear that after four-and-a-half years together, he would say to me: "Oh you are so mixed up."

I asked her why she thought herself mixed up. Again, on the edge of tears she replied:

This hits me every few months . . . I can't say why. . . . . . .

My grandmother survived, but died before I was born. At age two, I knew that something was different; I wanted a grandmother. So I adopted a Greek lady who was a friend of the family.

My own grandmother saved my mother during the war, and yet she physically abused her. After the war she remarried a man whom she met in a displaced persons' camp. This man was also abusive; therefore, my mother hated her stepfather. I think that my mother finds it hard to speak about this episode in her life, so that I am uncomfortable speaking about it, too. Thus I won't go any further on that subject. Both of my brothers knew my grandmother; my middle brother doesn't remember, but my older brother may have been almost ten years old. My father's first child died before I was born; everyone but I knew him. Again, this is a world that I never experienced, and yet it works on my subconscious, just like being second generation, and I want to know.

I went to a Montessori school from kindergarten to the fifth grade; except for the third grade when I attended a Quaker school. Later on, I went to an Episcopalian school. I was the only Jewish child in the school besides, another child who was half-Jewish. I was stigmatized and teased, resulting in my feeling very Jewish.

Why is your Jewish identity primarily associated with persecution?

This is part of the problem with me. The reason why I am not a practicing Jew right now is because I don't believe in God in the Jewish sense. I firmly support the Jewish cultural heritage, because in Jewish traditions, action is the most important matter. To my mind, action defines everyone. My mother doesn't believe in God; my father is a Zionist, but not religious. His own father was very religious, and my father hated it.

I spoke to many people of the second generation at the conference. Some of them have become religious because they have been persecuted and that is their answer; it's an anchor for them. For me, this is an anchor made out of fear, which I refuse. Furthermore, I don't believe in an afterlife. I don't want to die young, but I think that it is false to decide to believe in something in order to deal with that fear.

At one point, after having spent a semester in Israel, I thought about making *Aliya*.[2] However, I am anchored in American life. Of course, I feel no association with the American Revolution; that's not my past; it is part of the history of the country where I live. I think of myself American in the sense of where I was raised, and my current values.

I have always looked up to my mother who overworks herself and pushes herself so hard. I think that I have imitated her too much, because I, too, overwork and push myself in the same way. My mother, the child survivor, is a role model for me. In that sense I am proud, but it's also a significant part of my identity. Often people are in awe when I say that I am second generation and that my mother is a child survivor. On the other hand, when it comes to my internal life, when I feel miserable about things, when I feel unhappy with myself, it is tied to guilt. That's when I feel negative about my identity. I wonder how much is really due to the fact that I am of the second generation. It may be something else, because many people have similar feelings.

My family is full of secrets. Sometimes they hide things because they have their own issues; they have their own stigma attached to certain things, which I may not have. I am obsessed about being honest regarding relationships. I have trouble disguising anything; I abhor covering up, concealment drives me crazy. My mother concealed things when she thought that I was too young to hear. In the family, matters continue to be hidden on my mother's side, as well as on my father's. I know nothing about my father's first son. Furthermore, the only reason why my mother told me about her medical problems was because I made her swear that she would tell me if she ever had such problems. Medical difficulties get concealed in the family over and over again. I wonder what the root of all this hiding may be.

I define myself by actions and by the feedback that I get from other people. They tell me that I am a good person, and I believe them. I also define myself by personal relationships, also by where I went to school. On the other hand, I feel that the problem with describing myself is that I continually look to other people for my identification. I know that my mother does this, too. People keep telling my mother how wonderful she is, and that is primarily why she feels that she is a good person. Also, just like my mother, I have a lot of friends. I imitate her in that regard; perhaps that's unfortunate.

I wonder whether I want to continue teaching, and if that profession is part of my legacy. I taught third and fourth grade for two years to children with families whose incomes amounted to less than eleven thousand dollars a year.

I think that I am cynical, but sometimes I feel that I am only realistic when other people aren't. Again, I think that the world is a dangerous place, and I remain extremely cautious. Yet, I plan to go on a rigorous back-packing trip shortly, to challenge myself, to test myself as a survivor.

Since our conversation, I have had the opportunity to read Debra's play, which she wrote as a junior in high school. I found it powerful and moving, and was deeply impressed by the sensitivity and understanding from someone so young. I hope that she will develop it further. I also learned that she married the same young man she speaks of in the interview. Thanks to the Internet, I had the pleasure of viewing some pictures of her wedding. Later, I also saw the announcement of the couple's first child, a daughter.

NOTES:

1. USC Shoah Foundation Institute for Visual History and Education, University of Southern California.
2. *Alyiah*. Settling in Israel.

SASKIA

*MY FATHER NEVER SPOKE ABOUT HIS EXPERIENCE.
NOT HAVING A PAST ANGUISHED ME TERRIBLY.*

Saskia was one of the members of the Belgian group to participate in my project. I had noticed something different about her when we first met; she conveyed an impression of optimism.

I am the youngest of my parents' four children. My father was a hidden child during World War II, my mother isn't Jewish. I believe that my parents met in order to have a family, since neither one of them had any. They had children right away.

My mother had a rather complex and catastrophic story. Her parents separated when she was very young. She went to live with her retired grandparents, but later she lived in the Belgian Congo with her mother, until adulthood.

My father's mother died during the "Exodus"[1] in 1940, after she was hit by shrapnel. I don't think that my father has any memories of her. During the Nazi persecution of the Jews, he was hidden with farmers, where he was extremely unhappy. His memories of that time are very bad. My father is the only one in his family who wasn't deported. Except for an aunt and uncle who survived Auschwitz and returned after the war, he lost his whole family: his father, his grandparents, other aunts and uncles, and all of his cousins.

After the war, my father's uncle Dolf, brought up and adopted my father. This uncle of my father married a woman whom I always took to be my grandmother; I called her Oma. The uncle came out of Auschwitz in poor health; he suffered from pulmonary disease. He died fairly early from cancer in 1961, and my father stayed with Oma. She assumed the role of his mother when my father was between eight and ten. It was always said in the family that Oma married Dolf in order to be a mother to my father. Apparently, she couldn't have children.

Did your father purposely look to marry someone who wasn't Jewish?

I think so. Also, after all he went through, I suppose that he didn't want his children to be Jewish.

Does he appear to be happy about it?

I am not sure. I have that impression because my mother thinks so; she and I have discussed it. According to my mother, my father doesn't consider me Jewish. I don't really know that for certain because he doesn't say it to me; he said this to my mother. I think that he considers it an accomplished fact. However, things are a bit complicated, as well as paradoxical, with my father. My two brothers were circumcised in the hospital at birth. My oldest brother is named David. Often, in Jewish families the oldest son is named David, and is circumcised of course; so, you can see the paradox. Circumcision isn't a question of health here, as it is in the United States. In Europe, the only people whom I know who are circumcised are those who are Jewish, of Jewish descent, or who have health problems, or some abnormality. Therefore, it remains very unusual. My father says that it's a question of hygiene; I think that there is more to it.

My father has absolutely no Jewish affiliation, no Jewish friends, and no connection with the Jewish community. However, he looks typically Jewish and his name is Isidor; he never changed it. My mother is of Catholic origin, but she doesn't practice, and isn't even baptized. I grew up with no religion at all.

My second brother's name is Stefan, as in Stefan Zweig.[2] My sister is named Noémie, which is a biblical name. I am the only one without a "stigma;" my name connects to nothing special.

It's a paradox that among the four of us I am the one who is concerned with the subject of searching for the family's history.

When I was twelve or thirteen years old, I joined a Jewish youth group. I had a classmate who belonged. She said to me "Why don't you come, too? When your father was in Antwerp he was a member of *Shomer Hatzair*.[3] So, I joined. I went to a lot of Bar Mitzvahs and weddings, I had Jewish boyfriends, and I went to Israel.

My father never spoke about his experiences, never. All I ever knew until a few years ago was through my mother. It was through her that I found out, when I was eleven years old, that Oma wasn't my biological grandmother. I was amazed and terribly shocked. This happened by chance, when my mother was straightening out things in the house. She opened boxes and found some pictures, which she showed me. She said, "See, this is your father's mother." I replied that it was unbelievable how Oma had changed; I didn't recognize her at all. "But that isn't Oma," she replied, just like that.

My parents were always busy working. My father is a pediatrician. During the day, he worked at the hospital; in the evening, he worked at home. He was never there to play with us. He sometimes took us to the pool after work. Occasionally we played cards, but that was later. True, my father was present, although he didn't pay any attention to us.

When I was very small, I was very wanted. I believe that I had enormous love from my mother. But from age three on, I was essentially brought up by my brother David and my sister Noémie. My mother had a severe breakdown and suffered from depression when I was four. I have no memory of my mother from when I was four until I was nine. I only remember her taking me once to elementary school. Learning to fend for myself became a practice. When I was six and a half, I started coming home by myself from school by public bus. I could rarely count on my parents when I was very young.

I find my family a bit peculiar. My mother severed her relationship with her family; my father never speaks about what happened during the war. It's as though my parents were the founders of a new clan, never mind who came before.

My mother always said that in my family we could always ask questions on any subject; there were no secrets, no taboos. This is very strange, because she never said why she doesn't see her family. In addition, my father's story was never discussed. Thus, it has always been very complicated for me. Not having a past distressed me terribly. I speak about it with my sister, but I have little contact with my brothers. When I embarked on my genealogical research, I explained to my siblings, as well as to my father, what I found. My sister said, "How funny that you are searching for all that; it's great that you are doing it, but it's not essential." My sister isn't troubled the way I am by the lack of knowledge of our family's past.

My rapport with my father has always been difficult because I wanted him to speak to me. Not until the past few years have I understood that I wanted him to tell me his story. Before that, I just wanted him to talk to me, to have some contact with me, especially in my adolescence. He is terribly taciturn, and has no social relationships. I think that he has difficulty forming attachments because his whole family perished and he was bounced about from one place to the next.

My parents have never had a good relationship. Every year there was the threat of separation. It was always my mother who imposed this rhythm of passion and crisis. My father has always been the stable element. He loves my mother unconditionally, in his way. In his life, there is his wife, there are his children, and now there are his grandchildren. There is also his work, but he has total loyalty to his family. When I was nine years old my mother told me that my parents were separating. She had made the decision; she could no longer stand it and she would leave home. I clenched my teeth, but I didn't cry, I never showed my feelings and I never broke the pattern.

My parents have stayed together. After all the threats every year that they were going to separate, the situation calmed down. The subject still comes up sometimes, but I don't listen anymore.

I have no memories of having played with my parents, I didn't even play ball with them. In school, I was a tomboy; I was terribly aggressive and bossy. I played ball a lot with boys. But as far as playing at home, and in terms of feelings, I will always have these memories; I am still terribly affected by them.

When I see my husband's six-year–old niece, I find her so little. Then I say to myself, "At her age, I came home alone on the bus to an empty house." I cry when I speak about it. When I see the niece who is ten, I say to myself, "At her age, I had to prepare dinner for my family once a week."

By age twelve, I started fleeing from my house. Once or twice a week I would stay with friends. I never asked myself why; it was my way of getting some fresh air. I have had this very strong inner strength ever since I was very young. When my parents weren't there, I went looking elsewhere for what I was missing, where I knew I could get what I needed.

When I was working on my doctoral dissertation, my advisor was absent because he was a dean; but I knew where to go for help and on whom I could rely. I manage my own affairs well, and I press forward.

In my adolescence, between the ages of fourteen and seventeen, my father didn't like my being away from home, and he complained to my mother. Yet when I was there, he never spoke to me. I said to myself, "Does he want me to just be there like a potted plant?" I think that he wanted us to talk, but he was incapable to admit it ever to himself.

I would steal things in class: erasers, pencil boxes, etc. I was caught, and then my parents reacted. They took me to a restaurant so that we could talk. However, as usual, each time they would summon me for discussion, it always turned out the same way: my parents would argue, and I would leave the room.

However, for our physical and material welfare my parents were always there. Yet with my father there was often something strange going on. My mother told me that he said that he could never take any pictures of me because my skin was so fair and my cheeks so rosy. Whatever this is worth; my mother has a way of sorting out information. There has always been a distance between my father and myself ever since my adolescence. Later on, the distance became much wider. My mother always played the role of telephone, which suited her fine, for then she could control everything. When I wanted my father to know something, I would tell my mother. Anything concerning my father was always reported by my mother.

I told myself that this relationship wasn't normal. I had to do something to make my father react. In my last year at school, or in the year before last, I tried to make him respond by only greeting him, but never speaking to him. He never even noticed. In any case, he never reacted.

Then things changed. I was in therapy and working at the university as an assistant. I had to read a memoir of my choice, and I picked one written by a young woman about hidden children. This reading triggered my first realization of the problem with my father. In this memoir, I read that in order to survive, the hidden children had to deny their identity. I understood that these people functioned on several levels. At times they would operate in a certain way and pretend that the rest didn't exist; at other times they would act as though the other didn't exist. Well, my father behaved that way, and I finally understood. I wrote him a long letter saying that I wanted him to tell me what happened to him during the war.

On Sundays I always had dinner with my parents. So the following Sunday, when I went to dinner, I expected my father to say something to me about my letter, but he said nothing. I was so uncomfortable, so anguished by his silence, that I couldn't even ask him if he had received it. I left. I decided that he couldn't and wouldn't talk, and that I had to find out on my own in one way or another.

In my parents' house there are two family folders: one, is my mother's and one, is my father's. They are both in a desk with other important documents. I must have noticed them when my mother was putting things away. We always knew that Oma had kept all the papers. She gave them all to my father ten years ago.

I went searching in the folder where my mother kept pictures and old documents in order to find the names of my biological grandmother and grandfather. My letter wasn't in the folder, but it was on my father's desk in a plastic envelope. I noticed it by chance, but I concluded that he purposely wanted it to be seen to show that he had kept it.

Thus, I started to do some research that turned out to be extensive and very complicated. I called the "Jewish Museum,"[4] and the "Museum of Deportation"[5] in Malines. At the latter, I found a young woman who works there with records. I knew of my father's aunt Blume who had survived and who had gone to the United States. But I didn't know if she was still alive; I had to find out. Thanks to the *Musée de la Déportation*,[6] I learned that this aunt had married and changed her name. I searched the Internet and found a number under that name in the United States, and I called. The woman who answered the phone was, in actuality, my great aunt, who welcomed me with open arms. Ultimately, I went to see her.

Then I said to my father, "How strange that your grandfather's name was Samuel (Schmelke in Yiddish) and your first grandson is named Samuel, too. So there was already a Schmelke in the family. I only heard of Saul (my father's father) and Dolf. But after Schmelke remarried, he had four more children: a daughter, Blume, and three sons." My father replied: "Listen, I have no memories, I am not sure, I only remember Blume."

Each time I would tell him factual details of what I had found, he started asking questions. Ultimately, I was the one to relate his own story to him because he couldn't tell it. I also realized that I did this research principally for myself; I needed to know.

I also discerned how pleased my father was with my findings. He said to me, "Oh, this is funny; in fact, it's good. Now I won't be dying an idiot." Thus, in his way-- since that's how he is --he told me how very important it was for him what I had found out, and that it had helped him. So then I posed some factual questions; I tried not to show how eager I was, fearing that if I did he may draw back. I asked, "Do you remember where you were hidden? With whom were you after the war? It's impossible that no one knows where you were hidden. There must be a way, I am going to try to find out."

I phoned the office of the organization *L'Enfant Caché de Belgique*[7] (The Hidden Child of Belgium.) I communicated with people who advised me to get in touch with contacts in Antwerp. My father didn't object, and he agreed that I could do the phoning. However, I could no longer find out where he had been hidden because the only two people who knew had never spoken about it. They were Belgian gentiles; one of whom was an associate of my father's uncle who hid my father with Flemish peasants. My father was horribly unhappy there; he spoke about it sometimes, but very little and in a piecemeal way. He said that he wasn't treated well, that he received less to eat than the others. And, since he had less on his plate, he always finished first. Then he spent the rest of the meal watching his hands and nails. He was hungry and cold; he only hoped that someone would come and get him. He was hidden there at least two years until Dolf, his uncle, and later his adoptive father, came for him after he survived Auschwitz. He also met his aunt Blume, Dolf's sister, who survived Auschwitz, too.

Dolf told my father that he had him hidden in that farm the day before the whole family was deported. I think my father carries a heavy burden of guilt because he was the only one who wasn't caught. Dolf also said that when he came to get him from the farm, there were problems with the peasants. My father has no further details, but he thinks that these people expected him to be a kind of hostage, one who does just about anything on the farm, and gets the least to eat. He also says that since Dolf was an honest and loyal man, it was out of character for him to not ever see these people again, or take him to see them. After all, his being there saved his life. Thus, the only reason that I can see for why Dolf wasn't grateful was that it had been a question of money, and the situation became unpleasant when he came to get my father.

So then Dolf, who had lost his wife and his two children in the death camps, raised my father. Oma, whom Dolf later married, and whom I always considered my grandmother, had managed not to be deported because she had false papers. I think that she hid by working as a domestic in a family. My father always felt that he had never lived up to Oma's expectations. He carries those guilt feelings as well as the guilt of having survived. An adopted child often doesn't meet the ideals that parents may have for their biological offspring. Dolf loved my father, but he was very severe with him. He never spoke of his own experiences; I believe that he was too traumatized to speak.

At first my father refused to look at the folder that I tried to read. The papers were in Flemish, so I asked him to translate them for me. I thought that it would be ridiculous to have them translated by someone else, since he knew Flemish well. Finally, one of the people in the group did it for me. She also translated for me report cards from my father's elementary school in Antwerp, as well as papers in Hebrew, which I found in the folder.

It wasn't by chance that I wrote my dissertation on memory. My research deals with amnesiac patients, and about retrieval of information. For me, memory and evidence are very important. I feel much better since I was able to obtain the data of my father's family. Yes, it's horrible that they died, but now I am able to tell their story. Now I know how and where my grandparents died. Well, I don't know all that happened, but I don't have a black hole hanging over me regarding the past. Now there is a family history. I know that they came to Belgium from Poland. There are very few pictures, three or four of my father's biological father, one or two of my father's mother; also one picture of Grandfather Schmelke, who was Dolf, Saul, and Blume's father, and one of his first wife, who died of cancer, who was Dolf and Saul's mother. There is one very large photograph that had always been at my grandmother Oma's. It is a picture of my father's grandmother. I wanted it and my father let me have it.

My thesis dealt with the problem of memory in amnesiac patients, or those who have suffered cerebral trauma. In the process of memory formation, there are times when new information is absorbed. As I already mentioned, my work deals mainly with research where information is recovered. At the university, I work in the department of neuroscience. My work will now entail the study of test scan imagery, which is associated with studies in psychology. I see patients and collaborate with people at the hospital.

What was most important to me was to go and see my great aunt in America. My father had never had any contact with her. I was in therapy at the time. The therapist, who wasn't Jewish, said to me, "But why don't you ask your father?" I told him that this wasn't done in Jewish families among survivors, one just doesn't ask. He replied: "You are the one who says that one shouldn't ask; you impose that law on yourself, and there is no reason. You have a right to ask; you have a right to know your history."

But for me the taboo was so enormous, it was so insurmount-able at the time--this was between five and seven years ago--so I told him, "But you don't realize what it means to have a survivor in the family, you can't understand because you aren't from that milieu." He got very angry; he wasn't at all pleased with what I had said.

However, suddenly a change came over me, and I said to myself, "This doesn't work, all I do is protect the whole family. It isn't normal, and I do have a right to know." It was then that I wrote to my father. Now I am no longer burdened with this taboo, this weight of not daring to ask. I still protect my father, but now his family exists, its members were alive. What is more creative, incomparable, is that I found my great aunt, it was one of the most wonderful days of my life, it was fantastic!

Although he doesn't say so, I know that my father is grateful. When he said to me, "Good, now I won't die an idiot," he was telling me, in his way, he was letting me understand that he is very appreciative. Both of my parents admire me. They know that I am resourceful, they call me the family's detective because I search for what I need to find. In actual fact, I moved heaven and earth to find my great aunt. I telephoned every person by her name in the United States. I took all the phone books; I went to museums; I met a whole lot of people. At the time, there were two women by the same name as my great aunt living in Antwerp, so their data got mixed up. I called people of the same name in Brussels, I researched the Internet, but I didn't have the right spelling. I knew that it might take me two years, but I was going to find out. It didn't take that long in the end.

My parents admire my determination and they think that it's great that I gave new life to this story. I am now thinking of doing the same thing regarding my mother's family, I'll do it little by little. I am writing my mother's story in order to establish a record somewhere. I'll put it in my parent's safe deposit box in the bank in the form of a letter addressed to my siblings. I'll tell them that it's there. That way, I don't carry this burden, and if something should happen to me, there would be someone else who would know. I must do this because the burden is too heavy.

Do you sometimes feel resentful because everyone is counting on your strength? Do you feel that you have no right to be weak?

Yes, I have those feelings. For instance, I never used to call friends when I was troubled. It took me some time before I was able to call on them. I do it now when I am in need. There was a period that was awful, when I was writing my dissertation. My therapist became ill with cancer and died. The last year during my thesis I was terribly stressed, I had headaches, moments filled with anguish, panic attacks. On top of it all, I found myself alone at home because it was a time when my husband traveled frequently. That's when I called a friend at 2:00 am. I said, "Are you coming? I can't stay alone." I had never done this before. My resourcefulness is one of my greatest strengths in life, but when I couldn't handle the situation any longer, I appealed to a friend. In other words, I have no constraints. This helps me a lot in my work. When I can't handle a situation, I ask for advice.

I still have anxieties. If my husband is one or two hours late, I already fear that he is dead. I have called the police and inquired about automobile accidents; I have called hospitals; I have been in tears. In the past when, due to a misunderstanding, my husband didn't come home, I needed to take a tranquilizer. The dead of the past are there and I have fears of dying, mainly in an automobile accident. I fear imminent catastrophes at any moment of the day. It's OK when I drive in town, but as soon as I drive fast in a tunnel, I foresee an accident at the next bend. When I emerge I am relieved, and I think: "Thank God, I had no accident."

But I love life, I love festivities, I need to see my friends, to celebrate, to laugh with them. I love to cook, to eat, I am very open, I get very enthusiastic. When all is said and done, I can say that I am a positive person, I have worked it all through. Yet I do have moments when I say to myself, "All this is worthless."

However, I am happy to be living my life in the present. Also, I no longer fall into the trap of imposing upon myself strengths without limits. I allow myself to be weak, too. It no longer disturbs me as it did during my childhood.

My research and success in obtaining the information regarding my father's past gave me great psychotherapeutic joy. As I mentioned previously, it also taught me that I didn't need to always be a pillar of strength, and to allow myself times of weakness. This genealogical research enabled me to restore life where it had disappeared. Yet, I still remain with the dead, ... I still haven't figured out how to rid myself of this anguish that has been with me all my life

I enjoy my work, but it is very demanding. Research is required, and the huge competition I face in my work creates insecurity. I would like children, but not right away. I worked very hard on my dissertation, the past two years were very difficult. Just now, I seem to be coming to life again. I have gotten detached from the story of my father and his family and, in many ways, from my mother's story too. I have never felt as well as I do now. I married the man I love, I am happy. I would like to enjoy this time a bit longer before having children.

Perhaps my work defines me in terms of its always present, necessary resourcefulness. It defines me because it is intellectual and I need to think and ponder. It defines me because I always work with people, I am not alone in front of a computer. I find the contact with the public easy.

You define yourself by your profession, your role as a spouse, as a daughter, as well as a Belgian?

Yes, as a Belgian absolutely, also, as an atheist--or rather, an agnostic. Sometimes I say to myself that it would really be great if there were "somebody up there." As far as creation is concerned, my husband is a geographer and he often explains to me, which mountains are old and which are new.

Couldn't a different power have put them there?

Now that I don't believe. I have friends who are anti-religion, but I have no such feelings. People who believe do not disturb me, that's their business. They have faith, I don't. I am simply against fanatics.

My rapport with my parents is much better now, especially with my father. I didn't understand him before, but now that I do, our relationship has greatly improved.

After a two-and-a-half hour conversation, our interview ended on this very optimistic note. I told Saskia that she would hear from me further.

Since our last meeting, Saskia has informed me of several developments. First of all, she is now the proud mother of a son, Thomas. In addition, in contrast to the past, her sister has become involved in genealogical research. They now have this interest in common and discuss it often.

She has also communicated to me these further remarks:

My pregnancy and the arrival of my child have had a flourishing effect on me. I feel calmer, more serene, and more confident in life. I am still stressed or anguished from time to time, but in no comparison with the former intensity.

Changes have also occurred in my professional life. I no longer wish to continue doing research at the university. I am studying family and couple psychology, which I love. This plan of study contributes to my sense of peace. In a few months, my contract at the university will be ending. I will then search for new work in the field of clinical psychology.

My work is of less importance to me now. At this time, I especially want to spend time with my family, and I would soon like more children. I am still in therapy. This endeavor helps me enormously, in particular, concerning the subject of transmission. What and how should one transmit? How does one avoid the reproduction of traumatic transmissions? I have spent a lot of time thinking about these questions these past two years. My son is now a little more than one year old, and he is of great help to me in this project. He gives me the courage and the reason to pursue this matter. With my husband's help, and just as my parents have done in the past, I struggle so as to spare my children, as much as possible, the weight of our family's history.

Nowadays I say to myself that in spite of the difficulties that I endured during my childhood, my parents succeeded in giving my siblings and me a much better life than the horrors that either one of them had to survive. Today I realize that they have tried to do their very best, and how well they have succeeded. I owe them my gratitude.

⟐

I have been informed that Saskia has two sons now.

NOTES:

1. During the German "Blitzkrieg" of 1940, when Germany invaded Holland, Belgium, Luxembourg, and France, the term "exodus" was coined, signifying the flight of the invaded countries' populations.
2. Stefan Zweig, Jewish Austrian author, 1881---1942, born in Vienna.
3. Shomer Hatzair, leftist Zionist youth movement.
4. Jewish Museum – Musée Juif de Belgique – Brussels, Belgium.
5. Museum of Deportation – Museé de la Déportation – The Malines Museum of Deportation and Resistance
6. Ibid.
7. Enfant Caché de Belgique. Jewish organization of former hidden children in Belgium, headquarters in Brussels, Belgium.

GÉRARD

WHEN I THINK OF THE NAZIS I SAY TO MYSELF:
YES, THEY DIDN'T ACCOMPLISH THE WHOLE GENOCIDE,
BUT THEY SUCCEEDED IN POISONING FOR GENERATIONS
THE LIVES OF THOSE WHO SURVIVED.

Gérard was one of the group members who came to testify. His mother had been a hidden child, his father a survivor of several death camps. He grew up in a small town in the heart of the Walloon part of Belgium. At age forty-three, of medium height, he was trim and athletic looking. Gérard lived in Brussels. He taught sociology in a school similar to a junior college in the United States, and also worked as a translator. I asked him to begin telling me about his childhood, followed by his adolescence, and early adulthood. Gérard was very animated and agitated.

For me, my childhood was a hidden time. I have been discussing that period of my life, and beyond, with a psychologist for several years. I don't see it through rose-colored glasses, not at all. In the first place, I was relegated to this small town where I grew up, and where I often felt like a stranger. This was for me synonymous with being locked up--in certain ways like a hidden child.

For instance, I didn't want anyone in school to know that I was Jewish. I was in no danger, as had been the case for the children of the previous generation when the country was under the Nazi occupation, this was twenty years after the end of World War II. But

I was the only one who was unlike the other children. Therefore, I dreaded attracting attention and being found out. When I was asked the origin of my name, I avoided the question. In addition, no one had ever heard before of a first name such as my father's; it was a Jewish name and sounded foreign. Therefore, when on occasion it was necessary to say my father's first name, I remember feeling my throat closing up. Furthermore, when I wound up with the other boys in the collective dressing room for the swimming pool, the fact that I was circumcised was simply terrible for me. Also, when sometimes boys came to play at the house and would hear my parents speak Yiddish, they told in school that we spoke Flemish in my house. Therefore, I was stigmatized as being Flemish. This town is situated in the heart of Walloon country and harbors hostility toward anything Flemish.

In the sixth grade I had a teacher who told the class that he was a prisoner of war in Germany during World War II. He spoke with much bitterness about that period in his life. My last name sounds Germanic, therefore he suspected that I was German. When he said my name, he would put an *Umlaut* on the "u" in it, pronouncing it *ü*. When he spoke of Germany, he would say, "the Germans are blond and blue eyed, just like . . ." then he would point at me and pronounce my name with the *ü*, putting the emphasis on the first syllable, as in spoken German. This was dreadful, really horrible.

I also remember when we had what was called *classes de neige* (snow classes.) In the winter, the school would leave for the mountains. We would have classes there, do tobogganing, etc. I think that I was eight years old the first time I went, and I remember that shortly before our departure, one of the pupils said, pointing at me, "You are a Jew." Then the thought that I was going to leave several days later on a school trip, when he knew that I was Jewish, terrorized me. I remember not speaking to anyone about it. But during the whole trip this boy continuously passed by me making the Nazi salute and saying "Heil Hitler." It was horrible, horrible! What I mainly recollect is a whole series of incidents of this kind.

I recall the sensation of something very heavy, very weighty in the atmosphere at home. My father was violent with me and I never understood why, never. Perhaps he couldn't express his paternal feelings, and this was a way for him to declare them, however badly. There was never any violence toward my older sister, or my younger brother, only toward me.

With the thought of Gérard's story about his teacher's mentioning his blond hair and blue eyes, I imagined that his father may have been reacting unconsciously to Gérard's coloring, and so I inquired about his brother's hair and eyes.

My brother's hair was light brown, but I am not sure about the color of his eyes. I don't think that they are blue. In terms of my father's violence toward me, I have tried to interpret his behavior. I told myself that he was a man who must have had to, . . . how can I say, . . . button up his feelings, as with cement, because he had suffered so much. As a father, he had emotions that he couldn't express as he must have wanted to, and this lack was transformed into violence. This is how I perceive his actions.

Having said that, I don't think that I was a very obedient boy, nor was I disciplined. However, in school I was very good, I worked well and was at the head of the class. At home, it was a different story. In my work with the psychologist, the following hypothesis became apparent. It seems that I rebelled against this dead atmosphere at home, this lack of life. I was a vibrant child, who wanted to live, but I was confronted with something morbid; therefore I manifested this undisciplined conduct. This is, in sum, my childhood in a nutshell.

Did your mother interfere and try to protect you from your father's violence?

No, and this is something that remains, in a way, incomprehensible to me. However, when we did speak about it on rare occasions, she expressed such culpability that I decided to avoid doing so once and for all. She has such inclination toward guilt, perhaps due to her time spent hiding in the convent. I don't want to hurt her. Thus, I avoid speaking about it. I believe that she thinks that she should have protected me since that is a natural reflex for mothers. Yet, she didn't interfere then, I don't know why.

I had seen Gérard with his mother, as well as with his sister and her family. He was affable and seemed content in their company. I also noticed how solicitous and thoughtful he acted toward his mother, who told me that he is an attentive and loving son. She also said that she feels blessed, for each and every one of her children is kind and devoted to her.

And when your teacher pronounced your name the German way and called you "the blond with blue eyes," did you speak about it at home?

I could absolutely never speak about any of that. I have some terrible memories and I cannot understand how a mother could have behaved the way she did on one occasion. For example, I was with her at the parents visiting time when she came to my school. There was this very demanding math teacher who had never given 90% to anyone, but I got 90%. I remember her saying to him in my presence, "What he does in school isn't of great value, since he is impossible at home." Thus, I saw parents not as allies. No, it was out of the question for me to speak of this. I kept it all in me and I suffered greatly. I felt different from the other children. Then, when I was fifteen years old my parents had the idea to send me to a Jewish youth organization. I stayed there for ten days. It was atrocious. I had hoped that there I would at last feel at home. But, exactly the opposite happened, for I was the laughing-stock because I understood none of the Hebrew. There were prayers for Pesach,[1] and I knew nothing. I was really the "goy,"[2] it was terrible. I remember that I felt within me an enormous despair. I was nowhere at home, nowhere. This feeling is still very strong and prevalent with me today.

So there is my childhood, my adolescence. We never celebrated any holidays whatsoever. In fact, I remember a terrifying conflict with my father. As a girl, my sister was more protected, whereas I was always the bad one. We lived in the same house that held the store located on the street level. During the Christmas holidays, she would put a Christmas tree in the store's window. In the evening of Christmas day, my sister and I brought it into the house, to be like everyone else. My father had such a fit, it was ghastly, and

I remember it well. We were entitled neither to Jewish holidays nor any other ones. Celebrations never entered our house; there was never any rejoicing. I cannot recall my birthday ever being celebrated. I only remember once they sang a little when I gave them as a present a record of Yiddish songs. Otherwise, there was no singing, and there was no laughter.

But your parents got along well, didn't they?

Yes, they did. But there was never any manifestation of affection, or tenderness, ever. I saw it only toward the end of my father's life. One other time, I saw them holding hands on the sofa. For me, this was an incredible image. My mother has a photograph showing them kissing. To me, the gesture was not spontaneous; it was for the picture. That is what I feel about it. I considered it extraordinary on my father's part. My mother was more affection oriented.

My father never questioned us, he never spoke with us, and there was never a gesture of affection. He never asked us about our report cards, he asked my mother. Contact with his children was nonexistent. His only communication with me was beatings. I recall how, on Sundays, he would eat before any one else, and then he would leave to go to play cards with some people he knew in Brussels. My mother would remain with us and she always seemed distraught to me, all alone in that hole of a town. Sundays were especially sad. So, I am absolutely left with nothing happy or joyous from that period of my life. As much as I search, I find nothing.

Your siblings' companionship?

My brother is much younger than I. As for my sister, each time we had common activities, we would argue, and of course I was always the one who was held responsible, and I would get the beatings. Therefore, after a certain time, she became an abstraction for me, as if she didn't exist.

There was company from time to time since there were two other Jewish families in town.

There was one family, but they were competitors because they, too, had a clothing store. They had a son my sister's age, thus two years older than I. As I said, there was a sense of competition between the families. As a matter of fact they stopped speaking for a time; later they found each other again. It was difficult; they were materialistic people who liked to boast about their son's accomplishments and their acquisitions.

When my sister and I were adolescents, we were brought to a Jewish "center for the young" in the heart of Brussels where, as if by chance, sex education courses were given. So we learned about human sexuality. I suppose that my parents decided to bring us there because they were incapable of speaking to us about the subject.

Did they speak of their past, did they tell you . . .

No, no, they told us nothing. But I do remember that when someone would come over, which was rather rare, my father would speak only of that, his past. When there were films or newsreels he would watch all of them; he did this until the end of his life.

Did your mother speak to you of her past?

My mother spoke of her past, somewhat. We knew that she had been hidden in a convent. When we were children, she took us there several times to visit on Sunday afternoon and we had *"goûter,"* afternoon snacks, with the sisters. It must have been explained to me--I don't know very well anymore--that these people had rescued my mother. It was an impressive place, with this large crucifix and all the rest. The sisters still wore habits. I found all of it very impressive. This sister would kiss us, and there was her stiff headdress, all of it very intense. In terms of my mother's parents, I don't believe that what happened to them was ever explained to us. I have the impression that I have always known, but I don't recall having been told.

Did you know that your grandmother tried to escape to Switzerland and that . . .

No, not that, but I knew that abominable things had happened . . . it is as though it were almost an obtuse knowledge, . . . I can't say. I don't remember anyone telling me, but I know that I have always been aware. I knew that the number tattooed on my father's arm was due to the fact that he was put in a concentration camp and that if I didn't have any grandparents it was because they had been murdered. Also, even though it was never explained to me, it seems to me that I always knew the reason why my mother was in a convent.

And did you know the sense of abandonment that your mother experienced when she found out that while she was in the convent her mother had tried to escape to Switzerland and was caught?

No. That I found out much later. But I would classify all these events as though they happened to a cursed family that was hit by strokes of fate; just like that. . . .Why, . . .how? Why had it befallen me . . .? This has always been my reaction, and it still is.

Didn't you meet and speak to other youngsters at the Jewish summer camp and at the Jewish young people's center whose grandparents were also deported and perished?

No, I had the opposite experience. I realized that there were Jews of my age who had grandparents, who had uncles and aunts. I said to myself, "What is this all about? Why don't I have any?" And so I felt even worse. I saw myself increasingly cursed. I had been under the impression that being Jewish meant having no grandparents, having neither uncles nor aunts, nor cousins. Then I saw, . . . so that I felt more miserable.

Was it as though you had been made to suffer?

Yes, perhaps in a way I really felt that it was a sort of malediction. I recall having had such a sensation when, on rare occasions, my parents, my sister, and I went to the seashore. I saw other families there and compared them to mine. I had the impression that we were a stranded, lost family who never found a comfortable place where we felt at home. I considered us a roaming family that had been marked by bitter fate, and who ended up stranded in this small Belgian town.

This is something that has oppressed and disheartened me to this day. I am sickened by the fact and cannot accept that my mother and sister still live there. Especially my mother, who is after all in a phase of her life where she should enjoy the maximum that life has to offer. I see this as a sort of self-imposed punishment on her part. She stays in this town where my father had had an opportunity to take over a clothing store. Before they moved there he worked like a slave for a boss. They could have left once he retired, moved back to Brussels or somewhere else. He died there in a Catholic hospital. It made me sick to see that, and my mother is still there.

Well, I came to understand matters, I am working things out, but all of this is still extremely burdensome, and very oppressive. Yet I felt it was my duty to research this matter. The day I became aware of this duty, it was terrible for me, because it was as though every refuge and every retreat that I had in life was crumbling. I had a terrible breakdown, which was also tied to the fact, that . . . I want to speak about this because I feel that it is revealing and significant.

I was in a relationship with an American woman who was also French and who lived in Paris. I had had a previous relationship that lasted seven and a half years, but I believed that this was rather a youthful bond, and therefore I put it aside. Neither of these partners were Jewish. This last relationship, which was for me the true love bond of my life, ended six years ago. What was terrible for me was that the breakup was verbally violent, and verbal violence can be devastating. These outbursts of violence were often on the phone, since she was in Paris and I was in Brussels, but they were in letters also. She wrote to me something that literally wiped me out, it destroyed me to the point where I had to begin rebuilding myself from that time on. Of course, she blamed me for many things, since she had trouble leaving, because she loved me, too. She wrote to me, "You hide behind your parents' story, and it isn't your story." I was repelled. In the beginning, it felt as though I had been stabbed in the back. But later, when I had the chance to think it over, I said to myself," She is right! This is terrible, but she is right!!"

This concerned mainly the fact that she wanted children. Having children scares me, it terrorizes me. Besides, she had a certain attitude, how can I say, . . . a constructive attitude toward her life. She was studying for a doctorate. I wanted to study for a doctorate as well. I started, more or less, but I could never build anything, and I'll explain later on why. However, she couldn't stand it anymore. She wanted to move forward, and she wanted to build something: a family, a career. Therefore, she had had enough of me. I am not someone who builds, I have trouble building. So in light of that she literally threw me over.

She had nothing to do with this story, this memory of the Holocaust, and as she said, it wasn't my story either. I know that since then she has married a Jewish man who has a university career, a not very brilliant one, but a good profession just the same, and with whom she has a child. I know that had I acted the way I should have, I would have a university career as well.

I teach in a school, which doesn't satisfy me, because the academic level there is not to my liking. Oh well, I have no pretext, but I know that I could do better. So after a while she must have said to herself: "With this guy I'll never be able to build anything," and she broke off with me and wrote this, and I was absolutely devastated, because I realized that it was true. Yet I said to myself that if she could have said this to me in another context in order to help me, it would have been advantageous, since she was right. But to tell me this at the time of the break-up, at the time when she rejected me, that was terrible!

Do you believe that you would have been open to such a discussion?

No, I think that I could not have listened, I am convinced of that.

Then she couldn't have told you, could she?

Well, maybe I would have been more open because I loved her. If she could have used a certain manner, I would have understood. But she sent me signals, which I couldn't get, I couldn't. The idea of building was something completely foreign to me. Why? Why... because I have lived, and I still do live, in a certain way, through memory. I often think that what happened might happen again and, therefore, what's the use of building? I have this idea that if humans were capable in the history of humanity to commit such horrors, they will do it again. When I see people behave in such a heinous manner--and the occasions are many--I say to myself,

"There it is. The day when the context will be appropriate, they'll be Nazis, or a new variety. It repeats itself regularly."

But when you see people who behave well, don't you balance evil with good?

I try to do so, but I can't, I just can't.

Perhaps you look for qualities in people that aren't realistic? Maybe you have an ideal in mind and you expect to find it in other people?

Yes, possibly. It makes sense to say that we are humans with strengths and weaknesses. But, to speak frankly, I don't have confidence in humanity. In the past I was a militant leftist at a time when I wanted to participate in the creation of an ideal society, peopled with humans who would refuse to participate in wars, in massacres. I do realize now that this was unrealistic, that one has to be able to accept human beings as they are, but somehow I can't.

Yet you have met happy families.

No, I haven't. I don't know if I looked for them, but I think that I have no luck in that regard. Again last year, I was among friends who have two little children and whom I considered a model family. I said to myself, "At last here is a happy family." Among couples I usually get on best with the wife, I don't know why. One night at 11 p.m. she came crying to my door because her husband had beaten her. Then I said to myself, "If even they commit such terrible acts, then there is no hope." It is true that I am now at 10,000 kilometers away from the thought of being part of a couple, of having a family. However, inside of me, like every one else, there is something that aspires toward such a goal, but I cannot trust.

You'll remember that I mentioned a book by Philip Hally entitled: Lest Innocent Blood be Shed. *This author had made a study of what had happened during the Hitler years and the people who perished. The experience of his research was so horrible for him that it led to his having a nervous breakdown, and he lost confidence in humanity. Hally's saving grace was the discovery of what happened in a Huguenot village in France called Le Chambon sur Lignon. He learned of the courage of the pastor and of his family there, and of the inhabitants of the town who together saved 5,000 Jews whom they housed and hid. The story of this village saved Philip Hally. He could again trust in humanity, and so he wrote this book. Subsequently, there was also a film by Pierre Sauvage on the same topic about Le Chambon sur Lignon entitled* Weapons of the Spirit. *I think that it would be interesting for you to read the book and to see the film.*

But I try. I realize that there were people who saved Jews. I have, after all, several years of therapy behind me. I also have gone through depressions, and I know what it means. Therefore I try, but it takes an effort to say to myself, "OK there are people who saved Jews, . . . there is this, there is that . . ." But I feel such pain. I have the impression that every day I see signs to the contrary.

And this struggle with myself is exhausting, because it follows that I observe that there are people one can trust, yet I think that the ones one cannot trust are stronger and more numerous. This is a very deep feeling in me. I believe that indecency is latent and only requires favorable conditions to come forth. But the beast, the *salaud* slumbers, though, maybe not in everyone. However, the day when conditions are no longer good I am sure that all this filth will again come to the fore. I cannot rid myself of this thought. Therefore I have no confidence, I don't trust.

Your comments bring to mind The Plague,[3] by Albert Camus.

That is why I use the word *salaud*, referring to Jean-Paul Sartre's *La Nausée.*[4] I can philosophize and even write. I wrote a novel on the subject, but I couldn't get it published. Now I know why; it had to do with the narrative. I believe that it is significant, from the point of view of the titles. There are two of them. The first one is, *Comme Si* (As If.) The central character tries to live "as if" he doesn't know all that he knows of the past. Then I changed the title to *Les Morts dans la Tête* (The Dead in the Mind.) I admit that it is a frightening title, but I find it fitting. The protagonists wants to live as if he can put it all in a corner of his mind and live normally, but he can't do it. These dead are in his head for good. I didn't choose this title, it just came to me.

When my girlfriend wrote to me, " You hide behind your parents' story, and it isn't your story," I said to myself, "I'll try not to hide, I'll try to act as if all that were . . .." Well, no. It doesn't work.

You need an environment conducive to such an attitude. I have met people here in Brussels who get along well, who have nurtured children. Granted, they are often people whose parents didn't suffer as much as yours. In life there are always problems, but one tries to overcome them. Here in Belgium, as in France, among people of the second generation, some say that they have problems, others claim that they have hardly any.

I find what you say very pertinent. I don't know why, but I always find myself with people who carry heavy burdens inside. Speaking of the two partners who have an important place in my life, they weren't Jewish, but they also bore a big weight according to what they had experienced in their families. Oddly, I have the impression that people who were hurt in life attract me.

Perhaps you find that such people would more readily understand you.

Of course, but there are times when I say to myself, as you mentioned, "Maybe I'll look to meet people who have a more positive view on life." I don't much care for the expression "positive," I find it trite. Life is much more nuanced for it to be simply "positive" or "negative." I have tried to move away from thinking like that, but it is as though I am always brought back to the same place, that's what's so terrible. I even saw it in my therapeutic endeavor, my psychologist brought it to my attention. We tried to find a word for it, and we found the word *loyalty*. I believe that this is the key, loyalty. One is loyal from the moment one starts to suffer, because they suffered.

I see this loyalty in you, as far as your opinions are concerned, as well. Yesterday in the group, I felt that you maintained in yourself a certain rigidity, because you had decided to be at a place and not try to get out. It was as though you had fettered yourself through loyalty to this rigidity of suffering, and of atheism, as though you refuse to integrate yourself into a different type of Jewish society because you are disappointed with Jews. However, in our conversation of last Sunday, you mentioned a desire to celebrate Jewish holidays. You said to your family, "Why don't we get together with people who celebrate Chanukah?"

I said that more for my mother's benefit than for mine, because I think that for her it would be more meaningful, since she must have had such experiences in the past. I don't feel this same lack; I cannot miss what I haven't known.

You say that you don't miss it, but you may want to experience . . .

I say to myself, "OK, I am a human being like every one else with my own rigidities. Yet, I understand that I am also in need of warmth, of joy. I always thought that since I was so different from everybody, I didn't need the same things, but that's wrong. I do need what others need. This realization is already a big step for me.

I watched Gérard pouring out his struggles across the table from me, often unable to contain himself, and therefore frequently interrupting my comments. I empathized deeply with his distress. I hadn't expected this lack of confidence in him, socially, having seen him to be quite comfortable and affable in such situations. Besides, he was an attractive man. He frequently took extensive trips on his bicycle, and had just returned from such an excursion, tanned and fit. He was also an avid tennis player.

Don't you want to open yourself to the chance of finding friends, or a community with whom you would have common interests?

In the first group to which I belonged there were people who wanted to celebrate some holidays, so we made a Seder.[5] Maybe it was Rosh Hashanah,[6] I can't remember exactly. We got together for the observance, but I felt absolutely nothing. As far as I was concerned, it was theatrical.

But you cannot expect a spiritual experience and enlightenment on the spot. It takes patience, study, investigation, and comprehension. One has to be open to see, to compare, and this cannot be done at once and at one time.

Speaking of cultural and intellectual influences that can be helpful, I say, why draw more from Judaism, with which I am not familiar or know very little, than from Greek philosophy or oriental philosophy? I happen to have Jewish ancestors whom I didn't know, who have handed down nothing to me. So why would I have a stronger attraction to them rather than to the cradle of Western culture, ancient Greece. I like reading Plato, Aristotle. This is the question I ask myself.

You need to discover the beauty, the joy of life in Judaism, because that is what Judaism is all about. It is not about suffering and death; it celebrates life. Certainly it is enriching to know Plato and Aristotle, to learn about many types of philosophies. But Judaism is your own tradition, it is some-thing that belongs to you.

Why "my own tradition"? I have in mind the words of the phi-losopher Vladimir Jankelevitch,[7] I believe that they are his. When he defined the "Shoah,"[8] he said that it was an attack against affiliation. We, the second generation, experience a penetrating gauge through transmission, and I find nothing coming from my ancestors, nothing. I never had the opportunity to speak to any of my grandparents. Even my parents, my father didn't speak, or hardly at all. In terms of my mother, well, she was brainwashed. Only the name is Jewish, or perhaps some physical attributes, or the food that we sometimes eat. Besides that, there is nothing! And I sometimes wish, contrary to what others say, that this obsession with perpetuating oneself, with transmitting one's legacy, would stop. I say, enough!

I understand that you don't want to transmit suffering. If you were to acquaint yourself with some of the great Jewish thinkers, even if you left out the faith aspect, you would discover great richness in your own tradition.

There is one thing that my father transmitted to me implicitly, and that was his involvement in communism, in internationalism. He was in the International Brigade,[9] and this I admire greatly. He was unhappy when the Soviet Union collapsed. When I travel and people ask me what my nationality is, I have a tendency to say that I am a citizen of the world.

You know very well that this is unrealistic, and that communism is an attractive idea, but that it doesn't work. All these ideas, such as, "citizen of the world," "internationalist," are all well and good. But if you study Juda-ism, if you try to open yourself up and acknowledge your tradition, you'll find that in Judaism one chooses what is . . .

But I don't feel that Jewish philosophy is part of me. My former girlfriend was at once French and American, thus a bit between two cultures. She had a "love-hate" relationship with the United States; I felt close to her in that regard. I had the impression that I was on familiar ground with her, that she was someone who "fell between two seats," as I always had. I mentioned that in the small town where I grew up, I felt forever the outsider, and that when I found myself in a Jewish milieu, it was the same. I never felt at home anywhere, and I believe that this is very important to note. I am presently looking for an apartment. Well, it's the first time in my life that, at age forty-three, I feel like finding a place where I can say to myself, "This is my home, even if I am not terribly fond of living in Belgium, and hope that I won't have to live here my whole life." In terms of culture, I cannot say:, "This is my culture." When I read the Socratic essays I find ideas that captivate me. But I can also find them with the philosophers of the enlightenment or with contemporary philosophers. These ideas are my culture.

Last night at the meeting as I listened to you, I thought of Montaigne[10] who said, "But you have lived this day, you live day by day and living is already a big and important task. Managing one's daily life is already an accomplishment."[11] You, too, have succeeded, you became an adult, you are intelligent, and you learned to think, to sort things out . . . . .

Well, I don't consider things like that because I distinguish between "living" and "surviving." I think that I have had parents--now just my mother--who doesn't live, but who survives. In many ways this is true for me, as well. On the professional level, I realize that what I have isn't negligible, I could have done better, but didn't because I was weighted down and trapped at every stage. Truly, I am tired of just surviving, I want to live. I have added up the things that I like, and what I have published already has to do with the Shoah, and I no longer want to write about that.

What you have done is important, you have published, you have documented.

I haven't published a great deal, but I endured such suffering over whatever I did involve myself with on the subject. I remember one particular conference that I participated in and where a woman spoke before I did. She was a camp survivor who had written poetry. She read a text that she wrote while in the camp as she was watching smoke escaping from the crematorium. I tried speaking to her immediately afterwards, but I remained mute, I couldn't go on, and I apologized for not being able to speak after what I had just heard. This was the kind of suffering I experienced all the time.

I took part in a conference on the topic "Supporting Memory." I was on the film committee on memory because I am very interested in cinema. During a year and a half, every two weeks, we watched piles of cadavers. This was my intellectual work and the topics of my publications. It seemed impossible to me to work on anything else. It didn't even occur to me to undertake a different line of work. I started translating books on the subject. Afterward, when I understood myself better, I studied literary translations. I have the impression of constant redundancy, as if things went out through the door and came back through the window.

I say to myself that I must open the windows wider so that air can sweep all of it away, because this suffering is impossible, it is madness. When I think of it in retrospect, I realize that my former girlfriend must have said to herself, "This guy is going crazy!" Before our breakup, my mother had psychological difficulties and had to be hospitalized. My companion went to see her. She must have said to herself, "He will probably end up the same way."

I decided to reorient myself; I got involved with living things. I started to write, to do literary translations, got involved in theater. But ironically, I often returned, to the same subject: the Shoah. My therapist regularly brought it to my attention: there was in me a tremendous gorge, it was dizzying. I had the feeling that if I rejected all I had done regarding the Shoah, I wouldn't have anything left in life. I no longer knew what to do. Suggesting to myself that I live with something different, created within me a vertiginous gap. I most probably experienced feelings of treason, infidelity, and disloyalty. Little by little, I regained control, and the chasm closed up. That's where I am now. However, I still find joie de vivre elusive. Furthermore, I never saw my parents experiencing any, joie de vivre, never. There was none as far back as I can see. I believed that for me happiness was forbidden. Now I try, but I have difficulty. I recognize that I have a lot of trouble in experiencing joie de vivre. That is why I say to myself, "Well, . . . if one cannot transmit joy in life to one's children, one shouldn't have any."

In order to find joy in life, it is necessary to find a milieu where one is happy. Searching for, and discovering, such an environment should certainly be within the realm of possibility for you.

I am not very gifted in such endeavors. I never find an ambiance, a surrounding where I really feel well. You heard my sister say yesterday, "The only place where I feel well is where we discuss our misfortunes." I experience similar feelings. I often say that what I have done in life is of no value. I had reached the bottom of the abyss, where I experienced enormous pain. But when one is at the bottom, one tries to resurface. Keeping one's head submerged, even while trying to take a few breaths of oxygen from time to time, still results in suffocation.

You could make a clean sweep of it and start over again with work that you enjoy. You said the other night that if you could chose now, you would do something artistic.

I know that at this stage of the game I cannot start a great career in music. Music for me has always been vital. My sensitivity in regard to music leads me to believe that I could have done something meaningful.

Have you thought about becoming a music critic?

Yes, but I think that writing literary translations is a sort of intermediary. One starts out from someone else's work. It's a task of rewriting and one avoids the anxiety of the bare page, while writing nevertheless. Furthermore, I find the work on the language itself very interesting. However, translating reinforces the antisocial aspect, which keeps developing in me increasingly; this worries me somewhat. I have difficulty in my social relationships. I have none that are easy or happy, they are always very conflicting, stressed.

I teach in higher education, but I don't have any intellectual rapport with my colleagues, none at all. In terms of the students, OK, these are people who have chosen a shorter course of advanced study because they couldn't attend a university. This impacts the creative level of the class, therefore I cannot fulfill my intellectual potential. I petitioned the appropriate government agency and asked to be given courses at the level that I am entitled to. For eight years, a Catholic party education secretary put only people who were in the Catholic union in teaching positions, and I am, of course, in the socialist union. Therefore, I came to this school after two and a half years of proceedings with the state council, you can imagine the way that I was accepted. That's how things work in Belgium.

Many people cannot fulfill their potential in their work.

I have some satisfaction sometimes. Some of my students aren't too bad, but the context isn't encouraging or stimulating. When I go to conferences, I meet interesting people who work on different topics, people who are confrontational; I find this extraordinary. In the school where I teach, all is shut tight; there are never any outside contacts. Everyone teaches his little course, and there is no interdisciplinary work. It is an intellectual desert. Going to meetings is very difficult when one isn't at the university. I asked my superior for permission to participate in a day's study. He replied that I wanted to go to this meeting because I was looking for excuses in order to avoid teaching. That is his mentality. He cannot imagine going for a day's study because one is interested, because learning and opportunity will improve one's course. No, to him going to a day's conference means that you don't want to teach your course.

I frequently have problems sleeping, so that I am often tired and cannot attend to matters that need my attention. The other night at our gathering of people of the second generation, I was surprised when one of the members spoke of her sleeping problems. This is often a subject that people won't speak about because of the fact, it seems to me, that there is an aspect of shame to it. I think that not being able to sleep is the deepest manifestation of a troubled soul. I've thought extensively about the meaning of not sleeping, or of sleeping badly. I believe that this happens when one trades sleep for vigilance. Of what is one vigilant? Of dangers that haunt us, that threaten us. I think that not sleeping well is not being able to let oneself go, to be confident. Falling asleep is letting oneself be captured by sleep, relaxing. Not being able to sleep is not trusting, fearing loss of control. There is something somewhere that triggers the idea of always being on the lookout, of being ready to react.

One might say that psychological or emotional loneliness should not prevent sleep. As a matter of fact, when I was with my girlfriend, I didn't sleep any better. Perhaps I always feared loosing her. I found it so very wonderful to know that she loved me and that I loved her. I said to myself, "This isn't possible, it's too good to be true."

But you really feared committing yourself?

Yes. Rather, there are many kinds of commitments. I felt committed in terms of my profound feelings for her. But when it was a question of taking the necessary steps in order to eventually live together, and especially to have a child, that I couldn't do.

You said that your companion had a love---hate relationship with America. Of course, she lived between two cultures, since her mother was French and her father American. This places her in a special category of people. When they are in Europe they feel American, when they are in America they feel European. In many ways, they find themselves enriched by this duality. People with this background often feel cynical toward those who don't have this experience, who cannot understand.

To me, people who have roots seem to belong to a different humanity. I have come to realize that the people with whom I associate are predominantly of mixed ancestry. People in Europe are more anchored in their soil. In Belgium, one can sense the inheritance transmitted from generation to generation among Catholic families, in particular. True, I also have a certain disdain for that attitude. Being envious of them would be saying a lot, but at the same time I tell myself that these people know who they are, they don't need to ask themselves this question constantly. One could attest that there is certain richness in querying oneself regularly regarding one's identity, but it is also destabilizing. I say to myself, "What's the use of being more interesting if it doesn't make you happy?" I often aspire to tranquility. When one is tranquil, one sleeps well at night. I wrote somewhere in my novel: "Why don't I have a right to the same well being as these people who eat well, who sleep well?" It's tiring, it's exhausting.

Did you ever consider doing a doctorate somewhere else?

I am under the impression to be orphaned in terms of my subject. I would have to start from zero, because I am no longer interested in all that I have accumulated. In terms of sociology, all that I have accomplished during my studies in political science was writing two theses. I have never done anything else.

I think frequently about a change in direction, a start in a new career. I have also considered France because I like the country very much. Also, I have come to an impasse professionally because I have reached the maximum that can be obtained without a doctorate. If I were to do a doctorate, I would begin on a different subject. My brother did it here and it took him four to five years. My former girlfriend was in Paris when she prepared her doctorate; she gave English lessons in order to finance her studies. If I were in the United States, I would give French lessons and do translations.

That sort of work is not paid well. It may help you along, but it wouldn't be a living wage. Foreign languages are not valued there.

I suspected as much. Yet, I feel that there is something here in Belgium that doesn't suit me. I discovered this during the proceedings that my union led on my behalf with the State Council. I was confronted by someone who had no length of professional service, no experience. This young woman who was given the teaching schedule that I should have obtained was of a good, well-established Catholic family. It was a matter of politics only, not of merit. I took this very violently. This is what happens in this country. On the one hand, there are the Catholic families, and if one isn't Catholic, one is confronted with obstacles on the professional level, on the other hand, there are secular Freemasons, and if one isn't of that category, well then, one has trouble getting ahead in one's career; merit is an afterthought.

In France, in order to become a professor, one has to pass an exam. Here, there is no exam, there is a diploma and a political party. There are also people here who are well integrated in the Jewish community; they know influential individuals. That, too, is an advantage. I, however, am neither in the one nor the other; this is a handicap. My brother is very talented in what he does. He is very appreciated, but he isn't in any political party, nor is he in the Freemasonry. Therefore, his career progresses slowly, and some day he may even be blocked. I have never sought the support of anyone, and that is a disadvantage. My family has, so to speak, an ideal of purity: we don't want to compromise and demand to be recognized solely for our qualities. There is still a lot of unemployment in Europe, and in Belgium it is difficult to get a job. I know people who have found work through the Jewish community. Since we are not affiliated with any group, we aren't a Catholic family, we aren't a Freemason family, we aren't in the Jewish community, and we are nowhere.

How then do you define yourself?

That's a difficult question. I often answer such a query with subterfuge. When asked if I am Jewish, I say that I am of Jewish origin. When asked if I am Belgian, I say that I have Belgian citizenship, and I often specify that my parents weren't born in Belgium, which of course has nothing to do with the question. Thus, I always resort to some qualification. In general, a human being defines himself by his adherence to his culture. I however, am on moving terrain. I often feel closer to what is known as "feminine sensibility." I am always surprised to see that among the people with whom I associate, I find that a large majority are women; I get along much better with them. For instance, there are more women in the group of children of hidden children, as there are in the profession and study of translations. I assert and accept a feminine sensibility rather than a masculine one. I am not attracted to men, but again, my sensibility leans toward the feminine, therefore I find there, too, an identity difficulty. So, who am I, who am I? A whole lifetime is not enough for me to know.

I gave a paper at a meeting in Denmark with my former girl-friend on the connection between Jewish and feminine identities--also about the parallels that one can draw between anti-Semitic and antifeminist speeches. It's very interesting to find that there are far more parallels than one would imagine. I found articles in American journals discussing films where often the face and the personality of the Jew is effeminate, weak, a bit cowardly, and more emotional than rational. In anti-Semitic literature, the references are unbelievably numerous. Thus, I started writing with the thought of doing a doctorate on the subject. I have accumulated a number of papers on the topic. I found a paper where the author shows how in the eighteenth century the emancipation of the Jews and the emancipation of women took place practically at the same time. The talk in Denmark brought many favorable reactions.

Psychoanalysis and psychotherapy are exploratory endeavors. I started psychoanalysis because I wanted to explore my persona. I tried to undertake with my father a project aiming at finding out who he really was. I realized that I couldn't even ask him any questions. As a result, I started my pursuit in psychoanalysis, aiming at the relationship with my father. I then asked my mother to question my father and to tape his answers. Since he died I haven't listened to the tapes, but I hope and plan to listen again some day. However, what is extraordinary is that I conceived the idea of traveling with him to Poland. This was part of an undertaking, on my part, whereby I wanted to try to get to know my father better, and to know myself through him. I was told so often how much I resembled my father. For me, I attempted this because I had no contact with him.

We tried going twice, and twice we didn't get there. First, when we were already in Prague, we came back due to my brother's illness. The second time, we had a serious automobile accident. We could never reach the town where he was born, where he spent his childhood. I am not superstitious, but I must say that this is certainly disquieting. This attempt was destined to fail, and now he is no longer here. Therefore I have nothing, because I never really spoke with him. So, who am I?

I perceive myself often, and here I weigh my words and I think that it's terrible, but when I imagine where I come from I see myself as a heap of cadavers. That is to say, my parents are here but they weren't supposed to be. I try to rid myself of that idea.

This is exactly what Hitler wanted to do. This is giving him another victory, or rather, the victory that he didn't have!

I know it well. But you see, when I think of the Nazis, I say to myself, "Yes, they didn't accomplish the total genocide, but they succeeded in poisoning for generations the lives of those who survived."

Many people had to surmount difficulties. Some are struggling still but they hope to overcome them. It's often a matter of perseverance and will not to get locked up in despair and in the past. One must search and say to oneself, I have a right to happiness and I will find it. Perhaps it cannot be done all at once; it may be a long endeavor.

One terrible image is always present with me, and that is that at the time of the "selection" in the death camps, if they had sent my father to the other side, it would have been over. But I resulted from his having survived and I cannot integrate the fact that my life sprung from there. Again, I feel that it isn't living, just survival.

Life triumphed and must be celebrated. At conferences of child survivors we dance, we sing, we extol our survival. Why should you be so down on yourself when you have so much going for you? You are healthy, nice looking, well educated, and intelligent.

When one cannot find one's way in life, one has difficulty thinking of oneself as intelligent. I mean to say that the picture that one has of oneself depends, after all, upon the degree of satisfaction obtained in regard to one's accomplishments. I am not happy with what I have accomplished up to now.

Our three-hour interview ended with my attempts to convince Gérard of his many attributes and his great potential for happiness in his personal life and his career. Since then, he has obtained tenure in the school where he teaches, but is still not happy there. In addition, he has translated several more books; he continues to enjoy that part of his work.

NOTES:

1 Pesach. Passover holiday commemorating the Exodus of the Hebrews from Egypt.

2 *Goy.* Yiddish expression meaning Gentile man.

3 *The Plague, (La Peste)* one of the most famous novels by Albert Camus, 1913---1960. Nobel prize. 1957.

4 La Nausée (Nausea), 1938, Jean-Paul Sartre, French author and philosopher. Novel depicting the diary of the main character, Antoine Roquetin, who was unable to conquer his freedom.

5 *Seder.* Ritual meal at Passover, when the Hagadah is read, chronicling the Exodus of the Hebrews from Egypt.

6 Rosh Hashanah, religious Jewish holiday celebrating the new year.

7 Vladimir Jankelevitch, *Philosophie Morale*, 1998, Flammarion, Paris.

8 *Shoah*, Hebrew expression referring to the Holocaust.

9 International Brigade. Foreign volunteers of workers, artists, and intellectuals who fought alongside the Spanish Republicans during the Spanish civil war, 1936---1939.

10 Montaigne, 1533---1592. French essayist and moralist.

11 "We say: I have done nothing today. What, have you not lived? That is not only the fundamental but the most illustrious of your occupations. To compose our character is our duty, not to compose books, and to win, not battles and provinces, but order and tranquility in our conduct." Montaigne, translated by Donald Frame. *Essays and selected writings*, p. 425, St. Martin's Press, New York, 1963.

DANIEL A

*I BELIEVE THAT IN SOME WAY I LIVE IN HIDING;
A LARGE PART OF MY SOCIAL AND CIVIC LIFE IS HIDDEN.*

—~ ~—

*Daniel A. was forty-three years old and an only child. He lived in
Brussels, and was employed as a social worker. His job dealt mainly in
educating young adults as well as full-grown adults. He was in a stable
relationship with a non-Jewish French woman. They had a boy age five.*

My grandfather on my father's side fled from Belgium during
the war to the south of France. He died there due to illness. This
matter is rather vague for me, I never really understood the situation. I assume that my grandmother didn't want to go with him.
She stayed in Belgium with their three children, my father, the
oldest, and his two sisters. All three children were placed in hiding, sometimes with families, sometimes in convents, I don't know
exactly. My grandmother was deported to Auschwitz where she
perished. After the war, all three children were placed in orphanages. In Belgium, there were different orphanages for boys and
girls, so my father was separated from his sisters.

My father had an aunt; a sister of my grandfather, who was very
poor. She was the one remaining adult family link. Also, a very
kind woman played a role in that branch of the family--I used to
call her my "adoptive grandmother." I think that she also figured

somewhat as an adoptive mother to my father and to one of his sisters.

The youngest sister, who was very little during the war, developed psychiatric problems. When I was a child she seemed to have had some sort of normal life for a while, because she was able to hold down a job. However, her condition got worse after that, she had a persecution complex; crisis of paranoia; she heard people speaking about her, saying that she is Jewish. Ultimately, she was institutionalized.

My maternal grandparents were deported and didn't come back. After the war, my mother found herself completely alone; she had no relatives. There was a large hole in her life. I am not quite sure about her siblings; apparently some of them died of disease before the war. There was another sister whom my grandparents took to live with relatives in a small village in Romania. This sister remained a mystery for my mother, she never knew exactly what became of her. I believe that my mother always harbored guilt feelings, believing that her parents abandoned her sister in order to take care of her, and that, therefore she was saved. However, my mother never told me that explicitly. The fact that she had guilt feelings on that account is simply my impression.

Through a network of the Jewish community my mother found a great aunt who had immigrated to Israel. She went to see her during the seventies.

Didn't your mother ever speak with you about this subject, as well as other aspects of her life?

I think that my mother tried to tell me things. But I was young at the time, and I wasn't open to listening to such "confidential" information. I was thinking of my own projects, and didn't respond to the timid calls of attention that she made. I didn't want to listen. Previously, however, probably subconsciously while I was growing up, I think that my parents dismissed all of what happened to them, as though nothing happened before my birth. I must have integrated this attitude.

My parents married because my mother was pregnant with me. They met at a young peoples' get together. I don't believe that they would have married had I not been on the way. They were already not getting along. They separated when I was thirteen years old. Neither my mother nor my father ever reconstructed a family life. My mother had several relationships, but never anything stable.

My father was a violent person. He would beat me as well as my mother. I remember that in my adolescence, before he left us, my father would strike me and then he would cry, and apologize. I knew that I was mad at him, not only because he hit me, which exasperated me, but also because I couldn't tolerate his crying after he struck me. I felt that by apologizing and weeping he prevented me from holding his violence against him. This was intolerable for me.

Did he cry after he hit your mother?

This I don't know. I don't think that he hurt her to the point where it was visible. I remember that once he struck me with a belt. He had moments of extreme anger, and whenever we spent a weekend together, we knew that sooner or later he would get mad. My mother always seemed like a little girl to me, facing the big bad wolf.

My parents didn't meet again for twenty years. My father saw my mother once more, right before her death. She was already in a coma.

My mother passed away in 1989. During the eighties, it was discovered that she had had a brain tumor since childhood. Ultimately it became cancerous. She underwent an operation that was only partially successful.

After her first operation, I became aware of the fact that I hadn't heard her story, and I thought that I might never have an opportunity in the future. So, I started to speak with her a bit, and I looked at photographs that I had never seen. Some were of her aunt, whom she had gone to see in Israel. I had never asked any questions, and this was the period when I began to understand.

In my opinion, my parents never grew up. Each one looked to the other to be an adult. They searched for father and mother figures, yet neither was capable of filling this lack in the other's life; they were two children.

At the last meeting of our group of children of hidden children, which you attended, we spoke of memories of childhood. I have hardly any memories of that time of my life. My parents erased their painful childhood from their memory, I also blocked out mine.

When I was between ten and thirteen, I remember thinking, "My father is impossible, and he is insane. In order to survive, I have to lie, to live clandestinely." This is how I grew up; this is how I was able to shift for myself. I lived my life, but I made sure that my father knew nothing about it. My mother was in some way my accomplice.

My parents had friends who were also children of orphanages. My father had a double nature. He could be very nice, very obliging. He did many things outside the house—but very little for us. Then, sometimes without warning, he would turn into a monster. He had often fights with people, and he never tried to give an explanation; we would just stop seeing them. I must say that I inherited this tendency. I also know that I can be very nice and helpful, then at certain times I get angry, and I am incapable of giving a reason.

I don't believe that many people came to see us, given the ambiance at home.

There was often disagreement between my father and his two sisters. When things were going badly at home, my mother would leave, and had bouts of depression. Then I was sent to stay with this Jewish woman who had worked as a laundress in orphanages. I had some friends, children of neighbors. I went to camp, to youth groups, but I have no good memories, I don't know why. I had no close relationships, as the others did. I believe that I was a difficult child. I liked reading; I took along to camp with me *Les Misérables*, by Victor Hugo. I didn't want to do anything else, just wanted to lie on my bed and read.

I don't believe that I discussed the Holocaust with anyone at school. However, as I said, I have very few precise memories about my childhood, be they from school, or elsewhere.

I think that I was an intelligent child, in any case, a child eager for knowledge, yet, I had problems concentrating and studying. I am still someone who is very inattentive; I cannot concentrate for very long. Also, at home there was this climate of violence, so that I didn't do well at school.

The students had to copy into booklets to be taken home the grades they received in the various subjects. I remember cheating; I would inflate the grades. The teacher noticed, and mentioned my dishonesty in front of the class. I justified my cheating to myself by the fact that had I not changed the grades, I would have received a beating at home. I mainly tried to have good grades to protect myself from my father's anger.

In my adolescence, I would steal. I have never spoken about these matters to anyone. Now, as an adult, I wonder if my attitude was not linked to the lack of satisfaction I received from my parents. I had to obtain for myself the gratification I was denied at home. I believe that this feeling remained with me for nearly ten years. It is only now that I start to wonder, to reflect. I ask myself what it was that prompted me to steal. Why did I need these little toy cars, or another motor scooter? The one I took looked better than mine because it had certain attachments, or could go faster. I didn't get caught, but it could very well have happened.

Could it be that you wanted to act out a clandestine venture, and thereby prove to yourself that had you been on a secret mission you would have succeeded?

Perhaps it gave me some satisfaction, but I don't believe that I was proud of it. At the time I had no feelings of culpability. Now I buy a lot of second-hand goods. This is something of a shift of the same kind, this wanting to own objects above my income level. Well, at least I obtain them in a legal manner.

When my mother came out of the orphanage, she went to work as a secretary in a Jewish enterprise. Afterwards, she worked at a Jewish school where she remained as secretary---bookkeeper. My father went to study in Switzerland through the auspices of ORT, which is a global non-profit, social and educational Jewish organization, founded in 1880 in St. Petersburg. The acronym stands for the organization's name in Russian.

Did your mother get a good education in the orphanage?

She would have liked to study psychology. I think that she started studying in the orphanage, or while she was a young woman, but then I arrived.

Did you ever ask your mother why you didn't attend the school where she worked? Would you have liked to study there?

I don't think so. Although I may have liked to be closer to my mother, this Jewish school was very big. It started with nursery school, followed by the primary and secondary grades. I liked being in a small public school that was located in a working-class neighborhood. There were many Jewish students there, children of hidden children. My mother remained in a Jewish milieu, but stayed secular. Her parents weren't practicing Jews.

Both of my parents worked so that there was always enough to eat at home. My father became more stable after my mother and I left him. However, he often changed jobs. He worked as an electrical mechanic, later he sold electrical goods.

We celebrated no holidays. My cousin had his Bar Mitzvah. I went to synagogue once, but I don't remember anything about it. The second time I went to a synagogue was when I prepared for my mother's funeral. I had decided that I wanted her to be buried in a Jewish cemetery.

Did you feel a lack of spirituality while growing up?

No, I didn't know what it was. The youth group of which I was a member until I was thirteen or fourteen was a secular organization. I believe that I only understood the group's purpose after I left it. It was named "Union of Young Progressive Jews." I don't think that I knew what united us.

Did you discuss this at home? Did your parents ever question you?

No. I may have discussed it later. But, before the age of twenty, I have the impression that I felt subconsciously the wish to bond with people of Jewish origin.

Do you recall any feelings of happiness and well-being?

No. It didn't worry me, but it is like a void. I recall something, yet I don't know if it really happened, or if it is a memory of a photograph. I see my mother and my father on a motorbike. I remember its color, I remember the place. I must have been two or three years old: my father was in front, I was in the middle, and my mother in back. I remember a feeling of security. Yet I felt often left out. When my parents didn't want me to understand, they would speak Yiddish.

Were you quick-tempered as a child?

I don't think so, but I know that I am now. I try to control it, especially concerning my little boy. I have already slapped him. I know that I get easily irritated, and so I make an effort to keep some distance. I am aware that it is unacceptable to strike a child, and that it is much better to let him be. This tendency of mine worries me a lot.

I attempt to have a close relationship with my son so as not to repeat my father's attitude toward me. We speak from time to time. My son is five years old. He asks questions regarding Jewish culture, and I try to answer him. I don't know what sparked this interest. I took him with his mother, who is my partner, to a concert of Jewish music. He loved the music, and that particular singer. We went twice, and bought records, too. He also says, "I speak Yiddish," then he says a few words. I don't understand what he says. He also sings in Yiddish. He is a perceptive and intelligent child.

In terms of my emotional life, I could never figure myself out. At age nineteen, I left my mother and went to live in group communities. We would rent a house. There were men, women, and children. I had some affectionate relationships, but I never built anything stable. Perhaps it is because of my parents' story. I had relationships with partners with whom I didn't live most of the time. I met my present partner, who is French and lived in France, when she was separating from her husband. All the while, I managed to meet someone else. As a result, she was available for me, but I was no longer reachable for her. I believe that subconsciously I created this situation. She continued living and working in France. We met this way for fifteen years; the fact that she lived so far away suited me fine. Then she came to Belgium, and we had a child. It is clear that had she not been here, I wouldn't be a father, nor would we live as a couple.

Now I am very happy that this child was born, but I was incapable of desiring his birth. I agreed to his conception to please her. She waited a long time, and she wanted a child. She finally said, "I am now forty years old, you have to make up your mind." She is a very sensitive person. This characteristic is also essential in her job since she works in psychiatry.

My father and I stopped seeing each other from my adolescence on. When I became an adult, I renewed our relationship for a while. After my son's birth, we became a bit closer. But my father, who had always been difficult and short tempered, got angry with us and didn't come to see us for two years. I called him, I wrote to him, to no avail. Then I suggested that we meet. At that time I was already involved with the group of children of hidden children. He and I had a long discussion. I told him that he was perpetuating the work of the Nazis by breaking family relationships. I think that this must have been hard for him to hear. It seems to me that, in his mind, we are the ones who persecute him. There are certain matters concerning my son that we find unacceptable. For instance, my father would bring a number of toys and give them to him all at once. The boy would run from one toy to the other unable to concentrate on the one that his grandfather wanted to explain to him, so my father would get irritated. When I explained to him the cause of the situation, he got even angrier. Perhaps this echoes back to his past.

We resumed our relationship because he was about to be hospitalized for heart surgery. Recently he had a prostate operation. He disapproves of the way we speak to our son. He finds that we treat him as an adult and that the boy is being spoiled. We had another row and he left, slamming the door. This was about four months ago. I have met him in the street since then, and we greeted one another.

Has he ever had any psychotherapy?

I don't know about my father, but my mother was treated in the sixties. I think that this matter drove my parents apart. I believe that they were part of a group, and that my father stopped participating. My mother kept on going and made some friends. She also met somebody. My father has always blamed the psychiatrist who organized the group for their break-up. He is angry with me, because he also holds me responsible.

I admit that I wanted them to separate. I felt that the situation at home was untenable. My mother spoke to me about it, and I let her know that I wanted to leave. I think that financially it was very difficult for her.

When you tried to meet someone else in order not to commit yourself to your woman friend, did you try to meet a Jewish woman?

I don't believe that I ever had a Jewish girlfriend. I don't know if this was on purpose. The woman with whom I live now isn't Jewish, but she is a cliché of the so-called "Jewish mother." She has a very protective nature.

My partner didn't experience the Holocaust. She is very helpful toward me, toward the family. It is thanks to her that I have undertaken certain steps concerning my Judaism. She pushes me in that direction, and supports me. She knows that it is important. In terms of Jewish culture, I suspect that she is better informed than I am. Also, she was instrumental in my undertaking the role of becoming my parents' parent.

My son isn't circumcised, neither am I. My parents did everything to assimilate me, to protect me from being Jewish, to avoid any danger. My son is named Yannoé. It is a name we invented. It derives from Breton. We have good Breton friends, and at the time we often went to Brittany, which we enjoyed very much. The name also stands for Noé, from the biblical Noah. My partner's family lived in a French village named Noé, about one hundred kilometers from Paris. She spent the best years of her childhood there. Hers was a troubled childhood too.

As far as my Judaism is concerned, I would say that it was nonexistent until my mother's death. She lived in a nursing home. She had been ill for the previous ten years. It was evident that she was close to death. She had about eight days left. When I found out, I moved in with her, and my partner joined me. We stayed with my mother in her room. It was a time in my life when we were the closest. I spent a lot of time with her and spoke to her a great deal, which hadn't been easy before. I believe that we repaired many things at that time.

She deteriorated little by little, until she was finally in a coma. We didn't want her to go to the hospital, so we made arrangements in advance with the physician, as well as with the home, that she wouldn't be moved. I had prepared myself by reading about dying. I felt that it was important for me to be there, to continue talking, even when she was unable to answer me. I wanted to know where she wanted to be buried. We said in her presence that we assumed that she would want to be buried next to her parent, but her parents have no grave. So being near her parents would be to be buried on Jewish soil.

Daniel had difficulties controlling his emotions. He swallowed hard to hold back his tears.

Her father was named Kohn, thus he was a descendant from a line of rabbis. In going through her papers, I discovered that my grandfather was a talmudist--it was written on his passport. My great-grandfather in Poland was a rabbi. I know that in my mother's family rituals were observed. In Belgium, synagogues manage Jewish cemeteries, but they are located within regular cemeteries. We went to see one of them one evening, after we bid my mother goodnight. It was outside of Brussels. We found out that during the war my mother had been hidden in a children's home nearby. The cemetery was locked, but we went over the fence. We found the site very beautiful, and when we returned, we told my mother that she would be going there.

Did she react?

Well, she was in a coma, but we spoke to her, we touched her, she held our hands. I think that she was interested.

As a result, I straightened out several matters. At the gravesite, it was very clear to me that this was the right place for her, and it was also keeping her with her parents and her sister in spirit.

My father came to the funeral. I don't know if he visits the cemetery; I don't think so.

How do you raise your child?

He attends a public school. His class comprises three levels: nursery school, kindergarten, and first grade. The students are for the most part of North African origin; their parents came most likely from Algeria, Morocco, or Tunisia. I don't know if there are any students of Jewish origin in his class. It's a very large school composed of many different cultures and nationalities. However, in Belgian public schools, there is religious education available. For the students who don't attend religious classes, there are classes in ethics. We would like our son to enroll in the course for the Jewish religion. Yet, I also hope that along the way he would learn about other religions as well.

Well, it is clear that I don't insist, I am secular and a nonbeliever, and so is my partner. Her background is Christian, but neither she nor her parents can be counted among the faithful. What is important to me is that my son learns to understand.

Does your partner have precise ideas on the subject of religious education?

No, but we would like the boy to be informed.

Do you think that a child should have a religious education that would serve him as an anchor?

My partner's family lives in France. We see them three or four times a year; they come to our house. My partner celebrates Christmas. I don't particularly enjoy those celebrations. However, they are important for my son. It is then that we all get together, whether for Christmas or something else.

I don't observe Jewish holidays. My son once went with my father to a Jewish celebration in the youth movement to which I belonged when I was a child. Once he was invited by my aunt to come to the synagogue. He fell asleep on the way when we took him. I found my aunt in the synagogue and told her that I didn't have the heart to wake him up.

He never experienced a celebration with the Jewish side of the family. We never had a meal together that underlines the tradition. I would like to do that if I could find a way to avoid the tension and quarrels that usually occur. If there were a stronger family cohesion, we could get together, even if no one knew what to do.

You could inform yourself concerning the biblical history regarding the Exodus. It's a subject about slavery, liberation, and freedom. It's the story that is read during the Passover meal. The small special dishes placed in the center of the table symbolize what happened. I think that this experience would be very beneficial for your son, and he would know that you informed yourself about your own tradition. He is still very young, but he seems so sensitive . . .

I think that I am ready to see what I can do. In any case, I plan to tell him a lot more than I was told. It's an opportunity for me as well.

I would like to come back to the fact that you never went out with Jewish women. Have you thought about that?

I think it was a way to protect myself, to avoid sinking into the same kind of abyss that my parents experienced. I lacked the fundamental bases that they were unable to give me. Many people of my generation find themselves in the same situation. However, I don't think that I made a conscious effort to avoid going out with Jewish women.

Were your parents never interested, especially your mother, in your friends, in the women you dated?

I am just now realizing how much my mother was plagued with worries about her own personal life. I suspect that she was either incapable of advising me, or that she thought that I should make my own decisions. After we left my father, I lived with her and her lover. I imagine that in order to leave my father she needed someone on whom she could lean.

I was an adolescent, and I was difficult. I think that I liked the man. Their relationship didn't bother me. He was a student in psychology, much younger than my mother; I think that he really loved her. In comparison to our life with my father, I preferred that man. It must not have been easy for him to live with a woman and her son. I don't know how I acted toward him. Ultimately, he left.

I was a lot more difficult with the next man. Apparently my mother had an immense need for love and security. She met this young Spanish immigrant at a nightclub. I was older already, and I couldn't accept him because I didn't feel that he was someone who suited her. He was very immature, so I couldn't understand what she saw in him.

She never remarried, but she had partners. The one for whom she left my father helped her. I don't know how many years they lived together. When he left her for someone else, it was very hard for my mother. That was when she met the young Spaniard. She then had a relationship with a married Turkish man; he wasn't going to leave his wife and children. I think that she sought these kinds of relationships because she didn't really want anything stable. Her first partner could have matured along with her. In spite of the age difference, he could have shared her life. He was an intelligent man with whom one could have interesting discussions. This can't be said about the others.

I don't know whether my father had any relationships, since he kept everything hidden. When he was hospitalized after having had heart surgery, I went to his apartment where I hadn't set foot for twenty years. It was in a terrible shambles, and I tried putting it in order. There were wardrobes still full of my mother's clothes, also things that had belonged to me--toys as well as a framed drawing that I had made. It was like a cemetery. I think that he had waited for my mother to return. He had hoped. He imagined for a long time that my mother and I would eventually come back.

After a lot of wrangling with my father, I convinced him to come to the hospital when my mother was dying. I sensed his reticence, as well as my mother's when I mentioned it to her, but I convinced her that it was important for me that we have a moment together. I think that it was important for all of us. We all held hands. After a decade-long illness, my mother died at age fifty-seven.

I have been in a difficult phase for some time. I realize that I am harsh toward my partner. I am, just like my father, self-destructive and apt to ruin what's around me. I want to control myself, but I confess that I don't try very hard. I know that I am often angry with my son, or with my partner, and I think it's unjustified.

My parents' silence regarding their lives continued to affect me in different ways. My mother had a neighbor, a Belgian. I don't know whether or not he was Jewish. She owned a house which she sold to this neighbor in *viagé*, which is a form of annuity. It is a sort of gamble, the agreement being that the seller is allowed to live in the house for the rest of his or her life and receives a monthly pension from the buyer. If the seller dies early, the buyer benefits, but if the seller lives a long time, the buyer loses money. Therefore the property is sold at a low price.

The doctor told my mother that she had between one and two years left to live. I knew nothing about this. She was in very poor health, her cancer had returned, and she needed surgery again. So she sold her house to this man for a "scrap of bread," so to speak, never consulting me, or asking me how to proceed. When I realized that matters weren't going well, I wanted to interfere, but she refused. I should have insisted, but I stayed in my role as the son, obedient toward his mother. My mother was no longer clear-minded. She was very ill, she couldn't sleep anymore. This neighbor became her persecutor. He pushed her to her grave because his attitude toward her was infernal. He abused her goodwill. She had trusted him, but he kept pestering her until she had a relapse. After her death, he forced open the doors of her apartment and emptied it out. I took him to court, but I lost.

This house is symbolic in terms of transmission from one generation to the next. My mother was unable to transmit to me the culture of her people. At the same time, she disinherited me of all her material goods. Unfortunately, by the same token, I was incapable of struggling in order to take for myself any part of the above.

I began some research regarding my maternal grandparents. I didn't go very far, but I found some information about my mother's siblings. I needed to find out when they were born and what their names were. I also went to Malines and checked at the Museum of Deportation at the former "Caserne Dossin," where Jews were assembled before being shipped to Auschwitz. There in the archives it was possible to obtain copies of German deportation papers. A woman employee explained to me that some people had sent packages and mail to my grandparents when they were at the "Caserne." I made some phone calls and found a man who told me that his father, who had been in the Belgian Resistance, had lived at that address. Unfortunately, his father had never told him anything and now he had passed away. My research stopped there. Nevertheless, it was important for me to find someone whose father had had a link with my grandparents, even though I came too late to find out. However, my mother never made any such inquiries. She wasn't able to do it. All the hidden children needed many years to get over their trauma, if they ever did.

After my mother died, I examined her papers. To my surprise, I discovered that originally she hadn't been a Belgian citizen. My grandparents were citizens of Romania, and sometimes Hungary, depending on the changes of the borders. My mother obtained her Belgian citizenship because she was left an orphan after the war. My mother was born in Belgium; I would never have imagined that she hadn't always been a Belgian citizen.

Before leaving my father, my mother had a nose job done. She did it for esthetic reasons. I also had it done when I was eighteen. I had an unattractive crooked nose. The operation was a birthday present. My mother's eyes and hair were brown. I don't know the color of my father's eyes. I think that he was blond when he was very young. My eyes are blue and my hair is light brown now, but I was very blond when I was small. My mother's hair was curly like mine.

Are you going to marry your partner, Sylvie?

(**Hesitation**) This is a constant question in the family. Maybe; I don't know. I have always had before me my parents' image; a couple, officially married, but who didn't get along. I think that Sylvie believes that it would be a good idea as far as my son is concerned; I don't think it is important. I have always struggled against conformity. I don't know, it may very well be because of my reluctance to commit myself.

I believe that in some way I live in hiding; a large part of my social and civic life is hidden. Sometimes it is problematic and it bothers me. I would like to put this matter in order. Yet, at the same time, my unconventional nature gives me some advantages. I now work for myself. I am building a house in order to create a home for my son, my partner, and myself.

Given that Sylvie isn't your legitimate spouse, doesn't it worry you if something were to happen to you?

I think that this is very important. I took the necessary precautions in terms of insurance. Before we lived together, and before the birth of my son, I had a good and stable job in Brussels. My companion who worked and lived in Paris wanted me to move there. I suggested that she move to Brussels instead. She could stop working, we could live on my salary. In order to live in Paris, we would both have had to work.

I am happy to be a father, but at the same time, I am not sure that I bring a lot to this role. In spite of my age, I am still not very mature. I retain some adolescent aspects in my behavior and in my points of view. In my work, I often assume important responsibilities regarding people who look after other persons. Yet, I lack self-confidence, I doubt myself. I wonder if my uncertainty concerning my personal strength is due to a lack of paternal transmission. I worry in terms of my son; I see his strength, but I always put him down with negative injunctions, "Don't do this, don't do that."

Sylvie holds everything together. She is the one who believes in life, I don't. For me, moments of happiness are always followed by and linked to catastrophes. I carry this notion that I have no right to happiness. I cannot tell you why or how, but I carry within me the feeling that being happy is dangerous, that it is always dearly paid for.

You said that you marked the date of the next meeting of the group in your calendar e.c, standing for "enfants cachés" (hidden children) but that you never speak of these gatherings.

That is so. However, yesterday I surprised myself by saying to a friend that I was busy the next evening, that I had a meeting. But this friend isn't Jewish, and I have told him that I am the son of hidden children. We have spoken of how Jews had to live during the war. He finds it revolting. I learned from him things that I didn't know.

My family continues to rip one another apart. I think it is because they remained children, psychologically. They cannot build anything together. Each one underwent terrible experiences.

My father never speaks. When I question him, he doesn't answer. My aunt no longer says anything, and her younger sister is confused and tells stories. My mother started to speak after she visited Israel. She told of her family there. She brought back--I believe for the first time—a photograph. At one time, I thought of going to live in Israel on a kibbutz. The communal life attracted me. I never reconnected with the family there. I don't know how to find them.

There are many ways that you can search for them. It would be interesting for you to reconnect with them, given that you have so little family. Your son could find cousins.

On my partner's side there is a cousin. However, I agree that if I tried I could find them.

Our interview ended then. Both Daniel and I emerged shaken from the experience. He had spoken for the first time of deep personal feelings. I remained troubled by his pain long after we parted.

NADIA

*I SPEAK NEITHER TO MY FATHER
NOR TO MY MOTHER OF MY PERSONAL PAIN.*

Nadia was the first person of the group in Brussels to contact me. She was then twenty-six. I sensed immediately her depth of character and her intense sensitivity. When she came for the interview at my hotel, she admitted to being anxious and nervous. I did my best to ease her mind. We proceeded with her testimony.

My father was a hidden child, my mother was born after the war. My father was a cleaver of diamonds in Antwerp. He is retired now. His parents came to Belgium from Poland. My grandparents on my mother's side came from old French Jewish lineage. The family had hidden in the "free zone"[1] of France during the war. My mother is an actress. My younger sister was born when I was three. We had babysitters very early on.

Between age three and seven, I remember that a great deal of the space in our house was occupied by my father's work. Besides cleaving on the upper floor, he also did lithography. On the lower floor was his studio with his canvasses. It also held a piano that belonged to his painting teacher. My father's paintings were all over the house. He sold some occasionally, but not often.

I believe that there was too much affection between my father and me. However, I have no memory of closeness with my mother.

It was my father who acted more like the stereotypical "Jewish mother." As a child, I was prone to fits of anger. On one occasion, I had such an outburst when I saw my parents leave for what I thought was some social engagement. I believe that these tantrums reflected my anxiety. Each time I threw such fits, my father would leave the scene and wouldn't return. I was disturbed by his total silence on the subject of my anger, provoking further aggression on my part. My mother said nothing. My father wouldn't listen. Both my mother and younger sister always remained passive. My sister tells me that she has no memory of her childhood before age twelve.

The family moved from Antwerp to Brussels when I was seven. One of the reasons for that move was that my mother didn't want to associate with the very close-knit Orthodox Jewish community there. My mother hadn't given her first born a Jewish name and thought that the name she had picked was Russian. The second born was given a Hebrew name, and I was always jealous of my sister's name.

I don't remember how old I was when I first learned about the Holocaust, it seems to me that I always knew. My father isn't exactly sure of what happened to his mother. He thinks that somehow she got out of the assembly camp of Drancy,[2] near Paris. My father's father was deported, but my father never spoke of him. He says that he doesn't remember, although he was about seven years old at the time. My grandmother, my father, and his sister who was four years younger, ended up in a city in the south of France where a woman hid them. I think that my grandmother never spoke of her experience during the war. She was seventy-five years old at my birth. I think that if I had tried questioning her when I was old enough to do so, by that time she would have been too feeble and distracted to answer.

My father's sister later joined an uncle who lived in Israel. She felt that my grandmother and my father had abandoned her, and she resented them. On the other hand, my father who always felt keenly responsible for his mother and could never break away, envied his sister's freedom. The same sibling rivalry is repeating itself between my sister and me. In addition, the matter of responsibility for one's parent has reoccurred in the next generation as well. I felt tied to my father, just as he had felt fettered to his mother, until he finally had the strength to break away.

On occasion, my father, my sister, and I traveled to Israel. My mother was working then, so she never joined us. My mother's sister and her husband, although Jewish themselves, are anti-Jewish, anti-religious, and anti-Zionist. My mother also feels ashamed vis-à-vis her sister, and brother-in-law. In terms of my aunt and uncle, it's a case of self-hatred. However, I don't think that my mother hates herself.

Communication with my parents was practically nonexistent. There were never any conversations with my father on the personal level. I often posed questions, and he answered that he didn't remember. He expressed himself in indirect ways by throwing his emotions onto his paintings, and into his writings. He never expressed himself in living experiences. He shows his anguish in his paintings, but he has never explained his distress to me. I believe that he destroyed the family with his canvasses; they surrounded us, and the enormity was unbearable. When I tried interpreting the paintings, he would tell me that I was wrong. Now I lack confidence in myself and I think that I never interpret correctly what people feel; I always doubt myself. Moreover, I never go to museums, I never look at paintings, because I have learned so well not to look at my father's.

When my mother was often hospitalized with psychological problems, my father put me in the role of the mistress of the house. When she returned home, she would be resentful to find her place usurped by me, albeit unintentionally on my part. My father also took me to Israel by myself. Sometimes the two of us would spend the night together on the beach. My parents never went out together. Now they do since my having left the house one year ago.

My father married late because he had become a replacement "husband" for his mother after his own father died. He often took his mother out. This, in a way, was repeated with me, when

I assumed in many ways the role of mother, or spouse. When, sometime later, I uttered the word "incestuous" to him, he called me insane.

I often wondered why my father didn't keep contact with the woman who hid him with his sister and his mother. At the time, she was a French seventeen year old who worked for the French Resistance. One of her other duties was to take care of little Jewish children whom she hid from the Nazis. She emigrated to the United States and lives near Chicago. I wrote to her, and when she answered I howled with joy.

I was fourteen years old when I went to see her for the first time. She was now named Kate. Her son married someone Jewish and the couple had a son. I realized that the visit didn't turn out well because I argued a lot with the grandson, who seemed resentful of the attention that I engendered. Kate had never said anything about her experience during the war, neither to her son nor grandson. One day I told the grandson about his grandmother's role in saving my father, aunt, and grandmother. The boy didn't believe me, arguing that one doesn't withhold such a story for forty years. Later, Kate and her grandson came to see my father when I was on a trip in Israel. The boy finally believed what I had told him when he saw my father weeping as he ran beside the train when they left. The grandson related the incident to me later.

As I said, my father never speaks about what is essential, what he feels, he only tells what's superficial. He never spoke about his experiences to me before I was fourteen years old, but somehow I feel I always knew. He later told me some details. He said that he remembers being in the south of France. He recalls fleeing and crossing the Pyrenees mountains on foot and in shorts in the middle of winter. When he arrived in Spain, he went into hiding, but he attended school. Yet, throughout his explanations he has always remained psychologically absent.

Due to my renewed contacts with Kate, she started speaking in schools about her experience during the war. Someone communicated with Yad Vashem[3] in order to obtain for her the medal of the "Righteous Gentile." The museum awarded her the medal--a certificate--and a tree was planted in her name in the museum's "Avenue of the Just." I went back to see Kate with my cousin, who interviewed her. I thought he didn't have the nerve to ask the right questions. His emotions got the better of him. He found it difficult, facing this person who might reveal unknown information. I didn't take part in the questioning, but I filmed the interview.

Although it took my father many years to follow me in my expeditions, he ultimately also went to see Kate in the United States. They talked of doing a book together about her activities during the war. Later, a filmmaker became interested and planned a documentary of her story. However, by that time I didn't want to hear anymore. I had tried for fourteen years, and had come to a saturation point. By then I wanted to go on with my own life and detach myself from my father, whose obtrusiveness had always stifled me. I had fought so that he would at least consent to testify in a filmed interview for the Spielberg Foundation,[4] to which he finally agreed. The same foundation interviewed my great uncle, as well as Kate. At the time I was twenty-four. I had come to the conclusion that my work in that sphere had ended. I had been the protagonist in the whole process since age fourteen, I decided to store the tapes of the testimonies on a shelf and henceforth concentrate on myself.

One day I discovered the book entitled *Souffle sur tous ces morts pour qu'ils vivent* (Breathe on all these dead people so that they may live) by Nathalie Zajde.[5] In this book I found a passage that resonated as especially true for me and my own feelings. The author describes an interview with a young man who was at the Cinema Rivoli Beaubourg, in Paris, on March 29, 1985, when a bomb exploded during a Jewish Film Festival. This young man, a child of Holocaust survivors, witnessed the criminal attempt on the lives of the members of the audience solely because they were Jews. This experience, the fact that someone tried to kill him because he was a Jew, made the young man realize, among other things, the reason for his pain and his search for understanding about his parents' experience. I am searching for that reason, too.

I often dreamed of having something happen to me somewhere in order to give my feelings a reason, a *raison d'être*. I have rationalized that I have no reason for my feelings because I have never experienced anything to justify such sentiments.

My father said that he remembers nothing. I have always had trouble believing this. Furthermore, he told me that he doesn't consider himself a survivor because he avoided being caught and sent to a death camp. As I said, he kept expressing his real feelings in his paintings, but he never explained his anguish to me. I would often get angry, and he would burst out laughing.

I never speak of my personal pain, neither to my father, nor to my mother. At home the family spoke about Judaism, but never about anyone's inner life. In the group that I attend there is a lot of laughter. It is a place of discovery and expression where people can speak of matters that no one who doesn't share the same background would understand.

I attended the first gathering in Brussels of "Hidden Children in Belgium" in the spring of 1995, but my father refused to go. Representatives of the second generation also attended this conference. The support group for "children of hidden children." was constituted in 1997 after the second gathering, which I didn't attend. I joined a few months later and have now been a member for a year and a half.

In the group there was discussion about passing "the torch," a notion derided by most everyone present. No one wanted to carry it.

We all carry the "torch," all of us do. It is clear that we bear it; we carry it on our heads. The question is: does one keep and transmit the torch in a black, negative way? One of the men in the group will say that he is incapable of transmitting it in any other way. I believe that I would achieve something different, because I have transformed this torch from the manner in which I received it, from the way my father passed it on to me. I hope that I will alter it. When someone says that he or she doesn't want to transmit it, it means that this person would like to set it down for a while, build his life, and then pick it up again as his own, take it in hand, because he doesn't want it on his head. However, one cannot dispense with this "torch." For me, it constitutes my life, my inner self, and my identity. I repeat that it should be recovered, transformed, and of course the Shoah must never be forgotten.

I wear a chain with a Star of David. It helps me understand and justify the pain that is there in my heart. I need to be Jewish because I am nothing else. Having my father's tapes is very important to me. Whether they are on my mantle, or in the library, I prize them. However, I don't want them to be the only thing. I want a positive, lighted "torch," not an extinct one. When I held it in my hand, in regard to my father, he wasn't interested. But as soon as I let it go, he picked it up. After nearly a decade and a half of near silence, of psychological absence, of being incapable to mourn, he is now keenly interested and wants me to continue to participate. I struggle to detach myself from his influence.

I would want to marry a Jewish man and have children. To me, perhaps the only way to have a living Judaism is by transmitting life. I am a practicing Jew, less for myself, but for the children I would like to have. I believe that my adherence would give them a *raison d'être*. I would want to raise my children in a positive type of Judaism. I couldn't transmit this on my own because a part of this Judaism is dead in me, in my family. Two people could construct something that would have sense, that would move toward life; that would rebuild.

Yet, I feel very much alone. The group is of great help to me, but I know no one my age that is a child of a hidden child. I suffer from anxiety in launching my life, my career. I am incapable of asking for help.

Right now I teach Hebrew to very young children. I have a diploma in psychology; I wrote a thesis. I would like to continue my studies, specializing in developmental therapy. I know that I like the field of psychology. That is what I want to do, just as I know that I would like to marry and have children. Studying psychology has helped me to understand, to find the terminology, to discover what is normal and what isn't. It had seemed normal to me to spend the night on the beach with my father.

Now I understand that it wasn't. It was also very helpful to me to undergo a year and a half in psychotherapy, where difficult subjects that pointed to various trains of thought and considerations could be aired.

I am happy enough living in Belgium, I like Brussels especially. Every time I leave, I feel out of balance. I also have great affection for Israel, but I cannot find my place there, nor can I tolerate the antagonism among brothers.[6] In theory I am a Zionist, and rather leftist, politically. In the United States I liked New York, but didn't much care for Chicago. In Canada, I was fond of Montreal.

Since our interview, Nadia and I have been corresponding occasionally via e-mail. She informed me that she is continuing her studies, and that now she has one job at the university and another one in a care center for very underprivileged young children. The youngsters are placed there either by a parent or by a juvenile judge; they sleep at the center. She said that some cases are terrible: there are abused children, children whose fathers have killed their mothers, and also children whose very young mothers have hidden their births. Some children never have visitors. Thus, Nadia's work takes place in a difficult context, but she feels that it is valorizing and satisfying, because these children need help.

Sometime later she also sent me the following information:

The project of the documentary film of Kate's story was to be realized and the people involved were to meet in the city in France where my father, his sister, and his mother were hidden. My father insisted that I accompany him. I dreaded the experience, but felt that I could not refuse. When the plans for the trip took shape, my father immersed himself completely in the planning to the point where it became an obsession on his part. In his mind, this was a common project for him and me. I felt that he tried to engulf me in it. My anxiety stemmed especially from the thought that I would have to face all these people who would be crying for the major part of their stay. I couldn't tolerate seeing my father cry.

At the site, I controlled my stress, which demanded enormous energy on my part. I cooperated with what was asked of me, but I avoided giving in to emotions of any sort. I felt neither sorrow nor pleasure.

My father contained his emotions when he took me to the building where he had hidden. He also showed me the church where he had taken refuge at a midnight mass during a Nazi raid. I viewed it all without any emotional engagement. I had imagined these places a thousand times. Ultimately, reality couldn't replace the images that all along the years transformed themselves for me into memory. The reality and the images that I had assembled in my mind don't enter into conflict, they simply coexist. Nevertheless, the images, I already had in my mind, are by far more powerful. They form something equivalent to a film. They are full of movement and emotions, they surpass the reality that was brought to me fifty years after the fact.

Nadia has reconciled with her father. She has published an essay and a poem and is working on a book.

NOTES:

1. Free Zone. France was divided into a German occupied zone and an unoccupied zone, in southern France, administered by the Vichy government.
2. Drancy. Assembly camp outside of Paris used as deportation site for Jews arrested in France.
3. Yad Vashem. Jerusalem Jewish Museum and Memorial to the murdered six million Jews.
4. Spielberg Foundation. USC Shoah Foundation, University of Southern California, was established by Steven Spielberg in 1994. See page 19 note 1.
5. Nathalie Zajde, psychologist, clinician, and researcher, University of Paris 'Souffle sur tous ces morts pour qu'ils vivent', (Breathe on all these dead so that they may live. Bibliothèque d'Ethnopsychiatrie. Editions, Pensée Sauvage 1993.
6. Referring to the antagonism between Sephardic Jews and Ashkenazi Jews in Israel.

DANIEL O

*I THINK THAT IN MY CHILDHOOD,
AND EVEN IN MY ADULTHOOD, THE FEELING OF
BEING ALONE, THAT THERE AREN'T MANY PEOPLE
THAT I CAN RELATE TO AT A VERY DEEP LEVEL,
HAS REMAINED PREVALENT.*

*When I returned to the United States, one of my interviewees gave me
Daniel O's name and address. He assured me that I would find his friend's
testimony a valuable contribution to my project. Daniel and I correspond-
ed for several weeks via e-mail as we tried to find a time and place to meet.
We finally found an opportunity when he was temporarily working in
Baltimore, Maryland. On my way by car from Boston to the Washington,
D.C. area, I stopped in Baltimore and met with Daniel in his office.*

I am thirty-five years old. I have been living in New York City
for the past four and a half years. My job here in Baltimore is now
temporary, but could become permanent. I do political work,
nonprofit management. This is also what I did all of last year and
what I am doing now.

My mother was a hidden child. I am very pleased that she wrote
her memoir. She wasn't eager or necessarily available to talk about
her childhood. However, she did make it a practice to be accessible
for me to ask questions, often leaving aside her own experience.
I grew up learning and knowing some of the circumstances of her

life, but certainly not in any detailed fashion. When I sat down to read her book I expected that it would be old news to me. But now I have the benefit of knowing her story.

A recurring theme in my life has to do with circumstances. Aside from my mother being a hidden child, which comprises a small community to begin with, my father is not Jewish. Thus, there is the element of a mixed marriage. That detail didn't affect me as a Jew in any way, because I have always felt intrinsically Jewish, it was just a sense that I recall having from childhood. I think that this was true even when I was very young, before I knew that a child of a Jewish mother is considered Jewish according to Jewish law. My father, who is retired now, practiced and specialized in child psychiatry for a number of years. I think that he had a great deal of influence on my childhood and my life.

In my peer group there aren't a lot of people who are immigrants, but I am an immigrant. I was born in Poland. Then we were in Italy for six months, waiting for entrance papers to come to the United States. I have lived in the States now for thirty years, but I remember childhood in Poland. I also remember the struggle of learning English. Again, this is another way in which my peer group is narrower. So, I think that in my childhood, and even in my adulthood struggles, the feeling of being alone, that there aren't many people that I can relate to at a very deep level has remained prevalent.

It was certainly easier during high school, when there was a reasonable size Jewish community peer group in Ann Arbor-- some of whom were also children of survivors. It was there that I really felt at home in my age group. Up to that time, I had felt more comfortable around my parents' friends, and around people who were themselves immigrants.

My brother is six years younger than I. He was born in Boston, where we lived for over a year. We also lived in Taunton, Massachusetts, for four and a half years.

Did the fact that you considered yourself Jewish, and that your father isn't, ever engender any unpleasant feelings or arguments?

There are a lot of father-son issues between us. He definitely had some problems. He has hypertension, and he suffered a heart attack in recent years. But when he was younger, he had some problems with rage. His short temper made him prone to physical and emotional violence. I can recall a number of instances where, during an argument or a conflict between us, my mother would bring up Judaism and anti-Semitism. Yet to me, speaking about anti-Semitism as a phenomenon was completely irrelevant and not apropos to what was being discussed. I remember the first time it happened, when it struck me that he was relating to me not only in a father-son matter, but also as a non-Jew. This happened in my adolescence. I can remember very vividly how strange I thought that was. It came up, maybe, a couple of other times. Yet, I don't believe that it was ever the original point of the argument. He would bring it up during a tirade of some sort, about a great many issues.

Did you ever speak to your mother about it?

No, I didn't think of it being an appropriate matter. I believe that my life would have been less troublesome if he were simply someone easy to hate, and I could learn to grow indifferent about it. But I have a great deal of respect for him in regard to some decisions and choices that he has made. I think that he deserves at least a modicum of credit for helping my mother come to terms with her identity. When they met as adults in Poland, she was still emotionally in hiding, she had never really mourned her losses. He was largely responsible for her beginning a cathartic process of grieving, healing some wounds, and coming to accept her own identity.

Sometimes, when a parent is abusive, the child has a tendency to speak to the other parent about it.

My mother witnessed the abuse. I have a lot of issues with my mother. In some way I feel that she failed to be a proper parent by not protecting her young children. She certainly failed me that way, and I think that she failed my brother, too, in that regard. It is difficult for me even now to come to terms with some of those feelings because, intellectually, I am very aware of the circumstances, and of the fact that she grew up without parents. So, why is it fair for me to expect her to know how to behave as a parent when she went through such horrific experiences as a child, herself? However, that doesn't change the fact that as a child I suffered emotional wounds because she wasn't capable of doing what I now, as an adult, would expect a mother to do in defense of her children.

At the end of her book your mother says that if she had left her Polish guardian and gone to Israel, she would have been a better mother.

I don't believe that is the case. Perhaps when I was younger I harbored some fantasies as to how life would have been different had she married someone other than my father. But the fact is that I wouldn't be who I am. Also, it's a bit of a bias on her part, perhaps having to do with some guilt issues, or with blaming herself inappropriately. It's very possible, if not likely, that she would have wound up with a man in Israel, a Jewish man, who had his own issues of abuse that he would have perpetrated on his family. So, there is no easy way of saying that if she had done this or that, then these other things would have been different.

I think that there is something else important to take into account. Her book indicates that the man in the family where she spent a great deal of time, and where she was essentially in slave labor as a baker's assistant, that man was abusive. Contemporary literature indicates that girls, who come from families where there is domestic abuse between the male figure and the mother figure, tend to wind up with partners who are also abusive. There is no denying that such a pattern had already been imprinted on her. I think that she blames herself needlessly on that issue. I don't believe that Israel would have been a magic bullet that would have necessarily solved the problem.

She feels that she would have found her identity faster.

I think that there are ways in which my mother has yet to deal with her emotional scars. It is unlikely that she ever will because of her age and her place in life. She feels bad about certain things and chooses to focus on them to blame herself, skirting other matters where she should bear some emotional responsibility. Therefore, she has never grown in that direction. She has identified the issues where she feels comfortable blaming herself. So she takes credit, blame, whatever you like, in order not to have to look deeper. I believe that the real scars that need work in order to heal are more profound. Had she accepted some of that blame in a healthy way, and then moved deeper, she might have come to better grips with her experience. In my opinion, she is too quick to say, "Oh, I was such a bad mom. I should have done this or that differently." In my view, it ceases to have an emotional connection. She is saying it, and I know that she thinks it, but I am not sure how emotionally connected she is to it.

What difference would it have made in your life had she looked deeper into her scars?

This is a tough one. I think that in a healthy family there is a point at which parents come to recognize their adult children, not quite as peers, but as adults in their own right. That hasn't happened in my family. I don't see my mother capable of seeing me as her grown son. She always sees me as her firstborn, her baby. Also, had she been more centered about matters for which she can take responsibility, blame, and credit, instead of wallowing in guilt for some of these decisions, she might have been better able to see me as an adult.

On the flip side of that, I am thirty-five years old, single, and childless. Sometimes I wonder to what extent I have really looked for someone who could be a life partner with whom I could build a family. I have asked myself to what extent I purposefully don't attach myself in order to withhold from my parents the joy of becoming grandparents. It's a heavy issue that I have trouble figuring out.

Have you discussed with your mother your feelings regarding her actions?

Frankly, I don't think that she is a partner for that kind of discussion. Whenever we see each other, she is very happy. It is very difficult for me to feel any kind of emotional intimacy with her in order to speak frankly and honestly, and deal with issues that may be painful or may hurt her. I always feel that if I were to bring up something unpleasant, she would take it in the worst of all possible light, and I would be badgering her with something overwhelming. There are no gradations of matters that I can speak of that might be unpleasant. If it is something disturbing, it will hurt her. And so, rather than causing her pain, I don't bring these things up, and there remains a wall between us.

I first learned about the Holocaust when I was in grade school, and going to Hebrew school. I remember an event at the Jewish Community Center, where I viewed photographs and a slide show. I recall it being discussed among the older kids at the Center. I also remember very vividly my father, mother, and myself watching war footage on our black and white television. My mother broke down crying, sobbing on the couch. For me, up to a certain point, it was information on television, similar to watching what was going on in Vietnam at the time, or Watergate. But when I sensed how emotionally tortured my mother was, I realized that this had a deeper meaning.

I began to ask some questions, but it was my father who really answered and amplified the information. I would question my mother very gingerly about certain things. She made it clear that she was available to talk about the subject. It seems to me that very young boys, as, I was at the time, are more interested in information gathering. My father was very good in giving the details of what happened during the war. I don't think that I was able to lend comfort to my mother in any way. It was always emotionally troubling for her to talk about these matters.

You left Poland at the age of five. Did you know that you were Jewish?

My feelings of identity and who I was weren't an issue for me, just as for a fish it isn't an issue that it lives in water. I remember that in Poland we had very close family friends of my father. There was an older mother and her unmarried daughter, who was about my father's age. They were Jewish and had a lot of Jewish ritual objects: Shabbat candlesticks, a Menorah, things like that. We lived in an urban center where there was still a good deal of physical material that indicated that someone was Jewish, rather than part of the dominant culture.

Did you watch them make Shabbat on Friday night, and did your mother do it, too?

I don't remember my mother being there when the woman lit Shabbat candles, but she may very well have been. My mother never did it in our house. Neither did she light candles when I was going to Hebrew school; perhaps on a couple of occasions, but it wasn't her practice. I may have asked her why at some point in high school. I remember saying the blessing for her to repeat. I can't recall if it was over Shabbat candles or Chanukah candles.

What did you see when you watched that newsreel?

Footage of the camps, I remember it very clearly; it was during the daytime and may have been on a Sunday. I don't recall feeling any emotional connection to the material that I was seeing. I felt only sorrow toward my mother's reaction and I wanted to comfort her. We were sitting side by side on the couch and she was sobbing. At one point, it was too much for her, she was overcome with grief and collapsed on the couch. I remember wanting to lean over, squeeze her hand, or pat her on the arm. However, my father pulled me away, giving me a look indicating that I should leave her alone. I understood that this was something very private for her; that I probably wouldn't be able to make her feel better.

I first questioned her about it around that time. I came to understand that there was something important in her personal history around this subject. I asked her if she knew what happened, was this where her family was lost? She didn't know at the time. We obtained much more information later. I asked childish questions such as, "Where were you?" She told me things about her little brother.

When did you ask about your grandparents? You must have wondered why your mother had no family.

I don't know about that. I think that it was because of the circumstances of our leaving Poland. We lived in Lodz, which I remember as my hometown from childhood. I never knew my father's father either. My father's mother was alive when I was a child, I remember visiting her often. I also knew some of my father's siblings. Therefore, at some level, I knew internally that my father had this family that was also my own, and that my mother didn't. That is something that I internalized as a child and didn't ask why--at least I don't recall ever asking.

I am not sure when I asked my mother about her own parents. I know that I was curious. No doubt, at some level I wanted to spare her the pain that my questions might provoke. I think that there was also an underlying confidence that some day I would learn her story and discover matters that I needed to know. I never felt impatient about it. Perhaps I thought that she would speak to me when I was older and would understand better. I harbored a certain inner confidence that at the appropriate time I would find out.

Once I questioned my father when my mother and my brother traveled to Toronto. They went to visit the people with whom my mother had stayed in Poland, who had immigrated after us. I was probably nine or ten years old. We saw the newsreel when I was seven or eight. Hence, by then, this had been a topic of some import in the household for a couple of years.

My father and I were together for an extended period of time, and getting on rather well. That is when he approached the subject. I remember having this conversation sitting at the kitchen table. He said that now that my mother and my brother were away, it might be a good time for him to answer anything that I may want to know. I think that he could tell that I was curious, but that I hadn't broached the subject out of sensitivity toward my mother. Therefore, he made himself available while she was absent. He gave me a lot of information. I believe that he opened matters up to me at a very appropriate time. This is one of the ways that I think that he was really a good father. Perhaps it was due to his training as a child psychologist.

I asked him about a lot of things, including his experience during the war, and how he came to marry someone who was Jewish. That was the first time in my life that I remember seeing my father cry as he recalled some of these stories. It was really very difficult for him.

He described something he had witnessed as a child. He grew up in a very small town, really a typical nineteenth-century Polish peasant village. Only one Jewish family lived there. They had one daughter approximately the same age as my father. He remembered seeing his schoolmates chasing her in the woods. These were people with whom he went to church and learned church doctrine. The scene that he described to me was, to the best of my understanding, probably a rape.

At that point, we already had had a discussion about male and female sexuality. I don't recall him using explicit language. He expressed himself in a manner that he knew I would understand, as I got older. He probably trusted that I would remember the conversation and comprehend what he had witnessed.

When he broke down and cried, he said to me that he had felt caught between two worlds, never feeling part of either one. He wasn't part of the Jewish world, but he identified with the victim. He felt alienated from his peer group who were his classmates, his countrymen, and his coreligionists. In a confessional, he asked his priest what he should do about it. The priest told him to read the Book of Daniel. I don't understand the connection, but I gather that out of the incident my father decided to marry a Jewish woman, and name his first son Daniel. This was a powerful story for him, and his crying punctuated it for me.

There were certain times in my adult life when I questioned the veracity of this anecdote. I wondered if he had perhaps been a participant, and felt guilty about it later. Or maybe he harbored feelings of culpability for not coming to the girl's aid. He could have felt blameworthy about a number of things.

Your mother was a child Holocaust survivor, and your father had seen certain things in connection with the persecution of Jews. Did that make you feel "unusual," not just an "outsider"?

I already felt distinctive, perhaps to the borderline of narcissism. I can reflect now on the ways I dealt with my wounds in childhood, and realize that those ways were healthy. But I don't think that I ever felt "special" concerning Judaism, my identification as a Jew, or the Holocaust. I had a lot of anger and rage as a child because I was the repository of a lot of my father's rage. I didn't know it at the time, but I have come to recognize it now. The Holocaust became the storehouse of my anger when I began to learn about it. I felt that an incredible injustice had been done, and some day I would grow up to participate in the righting of that wrong. I would be on the side that would be fighting the Germans.

How did you feel about the Poles?

I felt Polish. I identified with my father as a Pole. I knew the largely intellectual circles that my parents socialized with in Poland. Afterwards, they frequented with Polish expatriates in America and Canada, also largely intellectuals. Those were the Poles that I identified with. Even though I was a child, these erudite people spoke with me very much as a young adult. They questioned me about politics and were amazed at how much I knew about current events. They treated me as an individual in my own right. And they were Polish. They had left Poland either during the 1956 wave of immigration, or in the late sixties or seventies. Sometimes there were also Polish Jews, but often they weren't.

Did you discuss the Holocaust with them?

I would discuss it with Jewish kids of my own age. I don't recall ever discussing the Holocaust with adults outside the home until I got to be an adult myself.

Did you feel different from these other Jewish kids because of your mother's experience? Did you feel that you knew more?

Not immediately, but over time. When we lived in Ann Arbor, we were members of a conservative synagogue. Most of the youth group kids were children of academics. I felt very comfortable in this crowd. I knew that some of them had the Holocaust in their families' history. Perhaps not as close as I did, but in one way or another we were all affected by it, it was a shared touchstone. I was vice-president of my local youth group chapter. I started having contact with kids not only from Ann Arbor, but also from youth groups of the whole region. I felt that the value system was generally the same across the Conservative synagogue crowd.

When my family moved during my junior year of high school, my parents became members of a Reform congregation in Jackson, Michigan. There, I encountered for the first time in my life the mostly suburban, Reform kids, and values that were entirely alien to me. These kids were largely driven by material wealth, status, and privilege, to my mind not values that I associated with Jewish values.

My first real girlfriend was the daughter of a child survivor of the Holocaust. I think that the relationship grew out of this background. She and I became very close because we had this in common. At a certain level, there was an unspoken bond. We knew this information about each other's parent, but didn't discuss it much. It was as though we had both been initiated in a secret club.

Coming back to your early childhood, did your mother play with you while you were growing up?

Not really, no. My father played with me somewhat, mostly with sports. It was competitive play, he never let me win, never let me score a point on the basketball court, or in water polo in the pool. I had to earn everything. He often said, "If you can survive me, you can survive anything the world can do." That definitely extended to the way he related to me.

I never wondered why my mother never played with me. Not until I became an adult did it ever occur to me as an issue. I think that I knew why she didn't play: she simply didn't know how. She didn't have that inclination, that instinct. She didn't know what it was to be a child. She knew what her childhood experience was, but she never knew how to look and see the world through my eyes. She couldn't relate to me as a child who was growing because she didn't have a healthy experience as a child herself.

However, both of my parents played chess and bridge with me from a very young age. But that's a different playing. They were teaching. It was an experience to get me to grow and learn. They didn't come down to my level, but tried bringing me up to theirs.

My father never came down to play with me at my childish level, either. Maybe he didn't play as a child. I suspect this was the case.

Yet, now that I think of it, I remember that on Sunday mornings my parents would sleep in. When my brother and I woke up we knew that my parents would still be in bed. We were welcomed in to play on the bed.

My mother was always gentle and affectionate with me. She often asked me how my day went at school. But in my memory, I see her at the kitchen sink preparing dinner, or doing something in the kitchen, while I had that brief conversation with her. As a child, I assumed that mothers don't relate to their sons, fathers do. It became a gender issue for me.

As you found out about your mother's past, did you feel protective toward her, in a way "fathering" her?

Protective, perhaps, at some level, but that would have been vis-à-vis my father's emotional abuse, rather than in terms of the impact of the outside world. I never would have thought of playing the role of parent to my mother. Though in some ways, I became the adult in the household. I was the one who taught my brother to tie his shoes, how to ride a bike. I was sensitive toward him as he got older and entered various stages of development. He wasn't keeping up with his peers; our parents weren't paying enough attention to the fact that he was getting older.

There were times when my parents were very affectionate and loving toward one another; there were other times of turmoil and anger. I think that this affected me very deeply, it is certainly part of the mix of who I am.

Did you discuss with your brother your mother's past and the fact that she lost her parents?

Only when we were older. We discussed our mother's behavior and attributed it to the fact that she was a child survivor.

I remember asking my mother once, when I was home for a visit, if she would say that she was happy. She gave a lengthy answer, questioning the existence of happiness, which of course answered my question. It also opened up something much deeper; her sadness was more profound than I had realized.

In Poland, my parents taught me some hymns that they re-membered from their youth, such as communist pioneer songs. However, I don't recall my mother ever singing with joy, or by herself. Around holidays, such as Passover or Chanukah, she would hum the melodies to the best of her ability. I can say with certainty that never in my life, in my presence, did my mother ever burst out in joyous song for any reason.

While I was growing up, I wasn't aware that this was missing. But coming into adulthood, and seeing people in different settings, I realized that there was an absence of *joie de vivre* in our house-hold. I vowed that when I had a family there would be rejoicing and gaiety. There are lots of things to be joyous about.

I have been to a couple of second-generation groups, on occa-sion. In none of them did I really feel at home, perhaps because of the communities where I was living. They were largely people older than I. My mother was very young when she survived, and she was relatively older when she had me. So, I often found myself being the only person in his twenties in the room. Everyone else was either in their thirties or forties, and they had children of their own. They were children of adult camp survivors, not of child survivors. These were people who were successful in their career, they were in stable marriages, proud of their own children. Yet, they said that they often felt an overpowering sense of malaise. They believed that all the fights that one hears and reads about in the news were microscopic in relation to what happened in the Holocaust. Yet, horrors repeat themselves because the world refuses to behave, people continue to mistreat each other, and the ripple effect sooner or later builds up and explodes.

I felt that I had a lot in common with them in terms of the above-mentioned point of reference. But they spent most of the time in discussions concerning their children. They feared pass-ing this toxicity on to them. I wasn't at that level, being single, in my twenties, and still a student struggling to make ends meet and paying student debts.

I have always known that when it was time for me to get married it would have to be to a Jewish woman. It is very important for me to ensure that my children are raised in a Jewish home. It has always been a certainty for me that some day I would find someone. I am not above picturing myself as forty years old and not having found an appropriate partner. I might then go to Israel and find a woman somewhat younger than myself. I would make her understand that I have a lot of decent qualities: I would be a good provider; our kids would have dual citizenship. Women are most likely more sensitive than men; they sense levels of toxicity for different reasons. There are women whom I would seek out as potential mates who would exclude me from their radar because they sense this toxicity in me. I don't blame them. I find those concerns perfectly valid.

Would you marry an Orthodox Jewish woman? Would you become observant? Given the fact that this would probably be the only way that she would marry you.

Sure, if I felt strongly that she was the right woman to be the partner for the rest of my life, and the mother of my children. If she would have me, I wouldn't hesitate. She could dictate whatever terms she wanted regarding religious observances, and I would accept them.

Have you ever thought that not having found as yet the "woman of your dreams," and not having children, may be connected to a fear of being abusive yourself?

Certainly. Yet I think that this was more of an issue when I was younger. I had a number of long-term relationships in my late teens and throughout my twenties. I believe that I stayed in them long-term partly because, deep down, I knew each time that this was not a woman with whom I was going to have a family. It was a comfortable way to spend that period of my life. I didn't seek more fulfilling relationships, I wasn't ready to be a father because of that fear. I am no longer afraid, but I believe that I must be vigilant all my life.

I have friends who come from families that were expressive with their temper. When I was in my early twenties, I recognized that a great many artistic and creative people are partly inspired, driven, and motivated by anger. They channeled those feelings in a healthy way into creativity, they turned something potentially negative into something positive. I have done my best to direct anger in ways that are creative.

You met people who were worried about passing on to their children the malaise that they inherited from their parents. Are you concerned that when you have children you, too, may be passing on such feelings to them?

Certainly. Children are incredibly sensitive beings. They soak up matters at a level that adults rarely perceive. Children are honest and see truth. Rather than dread this malaise, if I am ever blessed enough to have children, I would speak about it honestly. Every time that I have imagined being present for the birth of my child, it would always be a moment of great joy. But knowing that these children were mine, some of this pain, this uneasiness would be passed on to them. Therefore, when they would be old enough to deal with the information, I would tell them about some of my mother's circumstances. They would learn about occurrences in their grandmother's and great grandparent' lives, and they would have reason to be proud of them.

My mother's parents got themselves out of the Lodz and Warsaw ghettos. They recognized what was coming and got themselves behind the Russian lines when Hitler's army invaded the Soviet Union. They had two children. Although it breaks my heart, I give them credit for being strong enough to make this courageous decision. One child was old enough to perhaps survive on her own, the other had no hope of survival without the family. They kept the younger one in the hope that they might prevail, but they maximized the odds by sending the older one away, that at least one of the two might survive. What a decision to have to make for a parent! These are the people who would have been my children's great grandparents. Therefore, no matter what malaise they may take on, I think that I will also be able to transfer to them a very central feeling of pride.

Did you ever not want to be Jewish?

Flat out, no! Never was there such a time, nor was there ever a question for me. I wasn't circumcised in Poland because it wasn't a smart thing to do. When we lived in a very observant community in rural Pennsylvania at some distance from Pittsburgh, Buffalo, and Erie, I was studying for my *Bar Mitzvah*.[1] The officials of the community told my parents that in order to be *Bar Mitzvah* at their synagogue, I would have to have a *Brit Milah*.[2] My father advised me of different options that the community had discussed with him. I could study where I was, but for the ceremony I would have to go to a Conservative or Reform synagogue in Pittsburgh, or somewhere else.

For me there was no question. Of course, if I am going to have a *Bar Mitzvah*, and if I am supposed to be circumcised, well, we live in America now, I have nothing to fear. Thus, I was circumcised at age twelve.

It's wonderful to be so secure in your feelings and in your identity, especially coming from a mixed marriage. Did you ever fear that what occurred with your grandparents may happen to you some day?

No. Yet I think there are some ways in which childhood fantasies never die. Therefore, I was always involved with the survival of Israel. I had friends who were militant in its defense. I spent a lot of time working with Peace Now[3] because I really felt that the survival of Israel as a state depended on choosing a route of coexistence.

I experienced some anti-Semitism when I was the only Jew in my western Pennsylvania junior high school. As boys gave each other nicknames, someone tried to pin the nickname "Polak" on me. It didn't bother me, I laughed at it. They could tell that it didn't affect me, and they looked for a name that would. Later, I don't know how, one boy learned that I was Jewish. At the next occasion he called me "Jewlak." I didn't respond, I also didn't get stuck with the nickname. At the time, it didn't occur to me that this was a form of anti-Semitism. In retrospect, I think that it was.

In my work, there have been times when the subject of conflicts between the African American and Jewish communities arose, when people lashed out and struck at my identity as a Jew. This was done in an attempt not to focus on the subject at hand, but to look for vulnerability. I have been somewhat understanding of that and haven't fought back against it. I believe that it's a source of frustration to some people that immigrants like myself are successful in this country. People often look for outlets and scapegoats. Frequently those people's ancestors had for generations been in slave labor. Afterward, they remained excluded from the economic bounty for which their forbears were in great part responsible. I was sometimes angry with the subject that was being discussed. Certainly, two people having a different opinion as to how a certain event should be organized, had nothing to do with being African American or Jewish.

In the past, I have considered making *Alyiah*.[4] I am open to the possibility. I have moved around a lot. Four and a half years ago, there were opportunities for me in New York, Los Angeles, and Israel. Had there not been a great difference in the opportunity, I would have taken Israel more seriously as an option. Even now, it's something that I still consider.

I am lucky to be alive at a time of incredible transformation of the human condition. What I bring to that experience is my Jewish identity, as well as my heritage of being a child of a Holocaust survivor. I consider myself a citizen of the world. I think that nationalism was an expression that approached mass psychosis.

The fact that I chose to bring my resources to bear on the side of Bill Bradley[5] rather than Al Gore is indicative of how I feel about geopolitics. Also, Bill Bradley's wife Ernestine is a German-born academic. She has written specifically about how her academic peers have a responsibility to speak about the Holocaust in a way they failed to do. This catastrophe will continue to have historical repercussions on German culture for generations to come.

I have met among people my age some Germans who in a healthy way feel no guilt, or responsibility for the Holocaust. As we get to know one another, they sense that I don't blame them personally in any way. We have had very moving and powerful discussions regarding their feelings about their countrymen. In addition, I have had interactions with Germans my age who are hypersensitive and oblivious to the sum of German historical responsibility. I don't mean them individually and personally, but the fact that this happened in Germany. When I get to know that about them, I find ways to get under their skin, and they react very strongly.

I went to Dachau[6] a few years ago when I stayed in Munich for a short time. I found that Dachau was antiseptic. I was offended. I have been to Auschwitz,[7] Birkenau,[8] and Madanek. [9] In some ways, Auschwitz is more antiseptic than Birkenau which has been allowed to be left in ruins with the original barracks, the gas chambers, the crematorium, and the railroad tracks. One can sense the state of what it was like originally. Auschwitz is almost a museum. But at Dachau it was almost completely unemotional, antiseptic, white. Also, the information given of what happened there was superficial.

When I was in Munich, I tried to find a memorial to the Israeli athletes who were killed by terrorists in the 1972 Olympic games. After a long search, I finally found a very small monument. The people who lived in the neighborhood knew neither where it was, nor that it existed. Many of them were offended that I was even looking or asking. They thought that I wasn't sincere. I politely said that I was looking for some memorial regarding the athletes who were killed. A police officer was extremely insulted by my question. The reaction of some people denoted that they were sure that no such memorial existed and that I asked only so that I could refer in an underhanded way to these terrible things that happened to Jews in Germany.

What did you learn by reading your mother's book?

I didn't know how close to Christianity her journey had taken her. That she actually wanted to be Christian when she was a hidden child, came as a surprise to me. It is something that I hadn't known about her.

Do you believe that it is a good idea to document what happened to the "children of hidden children?"

It is an absolutely necessary, and an incredibly important project. I feel a responsibility to testify. I give my mother a great deal of credit; it was a very difficult and cathartic experience for her to write her memoir. I give a great deal of credit to anyone who goes through that process. I am not doing it, and I am sure that most of the people whom you interview aren't doing it either.

How do you feel about child survivors who discourage their children to testify?

I think that everyone's journey is individual. There were things that my mother refused to discuss as to what went on in the household. I understand that some people aren't willing to reveal their painful past, and dissuade their children from participating in any discussion connected with their Holocaust experience.

⚬ ⚬

After two and a half hours, we came to the end of our discussion. I promised Daniel that I would keep in touch with him. Sometime later, he informed me of a very close relationship he had begun with a young American Jewish woman. A wedding took place and I had the privilege to be invited. I attended with my husband. It was a memorable ceremony and party.

NOTES:

1. Bar Mitzvah. In Judaism, coming of age celebration of boys at age thirteen when they become adults and are responsible for their actions
2. *Brit Milah*. Hebrew term meaning "covenant with God." Circumcision of baby boys at eight days old.
3. Peace Now. "Shalom Achshav" Israeli peace organization.
4. *Alyiah*. Page 19 Note 2
5. Bill Bradley. William Warren Bradley, former athlete, later Democratic senator from New Jersey. U.S. presidential candidate in 2000.
6. Dachau. Nazi extermination camp near Munich, Germany.
7. Auschwitz. Nazi extermination camp near Krakow, Poland.
8. Birkenau. Nazi Satellite camp for Auschwitz
9. Madanek. Nazi extermination camp near Lublin, Poland.

YIFTACH

SOMETIMES I HAVE GUILT FEELINGS,
I THINK THAT I AM AT FAULT, IT IS ALMOST A REFLEX.
I FEEL THAT I SHOULDN'T MAKE MY PARENTS SAD.

—◦—

Jerusalem was our first stop in Israel. We had the good fortune to be housed for one week on the campus of Hebrew University, in Beit Belga (Belgian House,) a guesthouse donated to the university by the Jewish community of Belgium.

We contacted a family whom we met when they spent some time in Boston on sabbatical leave. The man was a physician at Hadassah Hospital, and his wife was a social worker. We met at their apartment for dinner, and the conversation centered on my project.

"Oh," said our friend, "our head nurse was a hidden child in Poland, and she has three children. I am sure that she would like for them to testify. I'll ask her tomorrow."

Indeed, the head nurse of Hadassah hospital came to see me the very next morning. She had spoken with her children, who agreed to be interviewed. Both of her sons and her daughter came to see me. I chose to recount the testimony of the middle child, the second son, Yiftach, age thirty, who at the time worked as a guide at Yad Vashem.[1] I did not include Yiftach's sister testimony because I felt that beside being a child of a hidden child, she also had many other difficult problems.

The Red Cross sent my mother papers when she was fourteen or fifteen. That was when she learned that she had been born in 1941. The Jewish couple that took her away from Poland testified to the Red Cross. They were the only ones who could know. We are aware that she lived with a Christian family during the war. My mother remembers that there were children in the household. Yet she doesn't know exactly how long she was there: probably until one year after the war, when she was four or five.

One day, a Jewish couple came to take her away. We don't know how they knew about her. They told her that they were her parents. My mother remembers traveling from Poland to Belgium, where they stayed for two years. The couple quarreled constantly and finally got divorced. The man went to the United States, and the woman took my mother to Israel when the State was established, in 1948.

My mother was still under the impression that these people were her parents. She was sent to live on a kibbutz, where she was well treated and happy. The woman stayed in Tel Aviv. Eventually Sarah, who lived at the kibbutz, adopted her. At some point, the person whom my mother thought was her mother contacted Sarah and told her that all the documents were in New York, with the so-called father. The Red Cross documents indicated that her real name was different from the name of the man who claimed to be her father.

The German government accorded my mother a sum of money as compensation for her losses. This enabled her to study and to become a nurse. She never wanted to have anything more to do with the people of her past. She had a photograph of herself at age four or five, which appeared at a gathering of survivors. One day, a man who had seen the photo, called saying that he had a daughter whose looks resembled the features of the child in the picture. He came to see my parents. This was before DNA tests were available. However, he and my mother had blood tests that proved to be inconclusive. In spite of his insistence, my mother was unconvinced the he might be her father.

So many among the survivors hang on to every lead in their desperate attempts to find loved ones. This man had lost all of his family. Even though the evidence was cloudy, this man insisted on claiming close family ties with my mother.

When I was growing up, *Yom HaShoah* (Holocaust Remembrance Day) frightened me terribly. I knew that Christians saved my mother. Therefore, in the second grade, I wrote about my mother being a survivor. I always asked questions, and I still do. My mother was very reserved when asked. However, she answered to the best of her ability, she didn't keep secrets, yet she didn't bring up the subject. I don't remember hearing my parents talk about it. My mother avoided the topic, she felt that she had a happy life and didn't want to think about the past. Of course, she also had trouble remembering.

I had grandparents and family on my father's side, but none whatsoever on my mother's. Growing up, I didn't miss this lack of family because my father's family was quite extensive. I had aunts, uncles, cousins; we had *Seders*[2] with many people. Yet, not having any family on my mother's side made me feel different from other children. I had one friend whose mother was also a child survivor. Contrary to my mother, who would freely answer any questions, this boy's mother refused to speak about her experience.

Each time I question my mother, another detail comes to light. As a teenager, when I kept asking, she would get annoyed, saying that she had already discussed the subject. She would say: "Look, I told you, can't you remember?"

My mother is a very nice, positive person, very open. Yet, she is impatient, she likes to get on, to get things done.

As I grew older, I realized what a sad childhood she had, how often she was abandoned--losing her childhood, losing her parents, not knowing who her parents were, not knowing when and where she was born. However, she wasn't obsessed with her past, it was more we, her children, who were curious. Yet, she can't give us the information that we seek, because she doesn't know. We urge her to persevere in her search; we need to know what happened to her family, this hole in our lives needs to be filled. Occasionally I discuss it with my siblings.

I always felt that I had to be good to my parents, I didn't want to cause them any sorrow. I never made the connection to the fact that my good behavior stemmed from my empathy for my mother's past. Subconsciously, it may have been so. However, consciously, I wasn't burdened by her past. I simply thought to myself that I had to be good, always obedient.

My parents put no restrictions on any of us children, especially not on me. I could do anything I wanted.

My father didn't have an easy life, either, although his life was very different from my mother's. We didn't realize this until he started speaking about it, only within the last few years. He was in the siege of the city[3] when there was hunger in Jerusalem; he fought in three wars.

I don't remember my mother playing with me. My father used to tell me war stories. He told them wonderfully well. We played jacks with him, not with my mother

How did your mother's story affect your life?

I am very interested in the subject of the Holocaust. Of course, I work at Yad Vashem. My decision to work there may have some connection with this concern. My former girlfriend said that I was obsessed with the topic. According to her, I find significance in insignificant matters.

I perceive myself as more knowledgeable of the topic. I feel that I am a more sensitive person. But then, this sensitivity may just be part of my nature.

My brother and I always asked my mother where she was going and when she planned to return. I hated her going on night shifts. Was I afraid that I would be abandoned, or that she would disappear? Not consciously. My mother was abandoned several times. Did I take her experience unto myself? Again, not consciously.

I had no self-reliance as a child. However, my mother wasn't overprotective of me. My parents have a way of being protective without us feeling that they are. As I grow older, I gain more confidence in myself. I am independent but still attached to my family. My older brother was more independent than I.

Sometimes I have guilt feelings, I think that I am at fault. It is almost a reflex. I feel that I shouldn't make my parents sad. It seems to me that I never had a fight with them; maybe sometimes, in my teens, but not often. Our household was positive, I never felt sadness. My parents had a good relationship.

When I was a child, my mother's friends would come and play the piano and we sang, yet we are not a singing family.

Did you always want to be Jewish?

I never thought about it, it is a natural fact here in Israel. I never wanted to be anything else.

My family gets together most Friday nights for *Shabbat.*[4] When I get married, I'll have a *chupah.*[5] If I have a son, he'll have a *Brit Milah*[6] and a *Bar Mitzvah.*[7] Judaism is part of my identity. I don't have a good answer concerning the deity.

Did you ever experience anti-Semitism?

I was born in the United States because my father was sent there to work for the Jewish Agency.[8]

The family remained there several years. I went to Jewish schools. I always had a protected environment, so that I never would experience anti-Semitism.

When you have children, will you teach them about your mother's past and tell what happened to the Jews of Europe during World War II? Will you also inform other people?

That is my job at Yad Vashem. When I go on dates, the subject comes up quite quickly, it is important to me; I never tire of speaking about it. My mother is sick of it, but I never feel that I have exhausted the topic. Sometimes I make believe that it is a legend in order to escape the horror of it all, it is so unimaginable.

Some children of hidden children are angry with their parents. They are of two different minds: either the parents told too much about the past, or not enough. Many of them blame their own problems, marital or other, on their parents. They blame them for having transmitted their experience to them.

If I thought that some of my idiosyncrasies were due to my mother's experience, I wouldn't blame her. I like to be truthful with my parents. I feel close to my mother, at times too close. It took me a long time to establish relationships with women.

I look for women who are secure in their personality, and who are strong. These are my mother's attributes. She couldn't have succeeded in leading a normal life if it weren't for her strength. If I don't sense a woman's strength, I feel that something is missing. I think that my wanting a strong woman is an effort to supplement some weakness in me.

People say that I am modest. I like being that way because at times I may feel better than others, and I want to control these feelings.

How would I define myself? I am honest and truthful. I want to continue my work at Yad Vashem, as well as continue my studies for a Master's degree, concentrating on the History of the Holocaust. Perhaps, studying German would be helpful.

I want to be married and have children. I want to continue to be a good son and be close to my brother. I find it more difficult to be close to my sister, who is touchy, different, and often difficult. I think that it would be good if you could speak with her.

Our discussion opened some windows for me and set me thinking. Thank you for your efforts.

Notes:

1. Yad Vashem. See Page 85 Note 3.
2. *Seder.* See Page 58 Note 5.
3. Siege of Jerusalem. During the 1948 Israel War of Independence Jerusalem was put under siege by the Arab armies.
4. *Shabbat.* In Judaism, 24 hour day of rest starting on Friday after sundown, ending after sundown on Saturday.
5. *Chupah.* Wedding canopy over the bride and groom in Jewish wedding ceremony.
6. *Brit Milah.* See Page 105 Note 2.
7. *Bar Mitsvah.* See Page 105 Note 1.
8. Jewish Agency. International body dedicated to cultivating Israel-Diaspora relationships.

TSILAH

I FEEL THAT LIFE IS EASIER FOR PEOPLE
WHOSE PARENTS ARE NOT SURVIVORS.
THEIR BURDEN IS LIGHT, AND I AM DIFFERENT.

My husband and I were hosted by my son-in-law's parents on kibbutz[1] Alonim in the north of Israel. Tsilah and I arranged to meet there since she lived in a moshav[2] in the same area.

Our discussion took place in the living room area of our kibbutz dwelling on a hot June morning. She was twenty-nine and recently married. From the start, I realized by her manner and her speech that this was a disturbed young woman. She said that she was interested in participating in my study because she had trouble with her father.

Her bachelor's degree was in history and archeology. She wasn't sure whether or not she would continue her studies for a Master's degree. At the time of our meeting, she worked in a bookstore.

In 1938 at the time of the *Anschluss* of Austria to Germany, my then six-year-old father fled with his family from Vienna to Brussels, Belgium. During the Nazi occupation and the persecution of the Jews, they hid with a Belgian gentile family. However, someone denounced them, and the Nazis came and took my father's mother and his sister. My father was saved because the man who harbored the family was able to rescue him, he said that my father was his son. I don't know the details about my grandfather. I was told that he was taken to a work camp.

My mother was born in Israel. When I was much younger, I heard things from her about my father's experience. I fantasized a lot about it. I am named after his grandmother. My name isn't very common in Israel. I wanted to know why I was named after her, but no one ever told me.

While growing up, I sometimes questioned my father, but he didn't like to talk about his experiences, it upset him. But now he would like to discuss it, though at the same time he remains very inward. On the other hand, he made a family tree, so in a way he established a connection with his past.

I was angry with my father because he always refused to tell me his story. I had heard of Mengele and the experiments he conducted on the children in the camps. I always thought that my father had not suffered so much because he was hidden, he was not in any of the camps.

I think that my father was unable to do what he should have done with his life because of his childhood. However, I could not accept the fact that when he behaved badly, people always excused him because of his past.

In 1993, when I was twenty-two, there was a Conference in Jerusalem about hidden children. I accompanied my parents to this conference. My father met many of the former children who, were hidden in the same monastery he was. At the sight of their delight at their meeting, I could picture them as little children. It was so touching, I nearly wept. They reacted to my empathy by hugging me.

I also joined my parents the day the conference went to Yad Vashem.[3] At the memorial ceremony, a woman explained to me the mental anguish that the hidden children experienced, especially those who remained the sole survivors of their families. I then understood their affliction. However, I didn't try to speak to my father, because I was hurt when he left me standing there and went off with his fellow hidden children from the monastery.

Before you went to Yad Vashem, did you ever mention to your mother that you thought that your father hadn't suffered very much?

No, I thought about it, but I never voiced those feelings to anyone. I am the third child, but among my four sisters, I alone am concerned with the subject. My siblings wonder why I consider myself "second generation."

A year after the conference I heard of a meeting at Amcha.[4] My parent's relationship was deteriorating so I asked them both to join me there. My father didn't want to come, but he relented and he finally came. There were people there from the second and third generation; everyone wanted to speak. I spoke at the meeting and said that I felt so awful. My father named me after his grandmother, but I knew nothing about her, and I think he should talk to me about her.

He found my remarks hurtful. I overheard him saying to some people, "Sometimes there is one child with whom the relationship is difficult, and for me this is the one." He gets along with all my sisters. They don't question his past.

After that incident I asked him to meet a psychologist with me. We went to one two-hour session, but he refused to attend any more. He cannot tolerate any criticism, he gets irritated very easily. If I asked certain questions, some inadvertent remarks in my queries would trigger something in him and he would get angry.

He never underwent counseling, he doesn't believe in it. When I was fifteen, my mother sent me to a psychologist. When my father took me there, he would say: "Oh, today you are going to the psychologist!" Intimating by his tone of voice that I was going there because I was kind of crazy.

I think that your father is an unhappy man, and a lot of it has to do with his past. You must remember that as a youngster he had no parents. In such a case it is difficult for an individual to be a parent because that person had no role model.

His father survived, but he didn't treat him well. He got married again to a harsh woman.

That is very sad. What happened to him after the Belgian man saved him by saying that he was his son?

The man's wife took him by train to her aunt who put him in a Catholic school. I told my father that I wanted to go with him to Belgium to see where he had hidden. He said that we should wait until my youngest sister completes her service in the army, then we would all go together. I think that he finds it difficult to be alone with me. He is afraid because I am very honest and he feels that he has to protect himself. He has a tendency to lie, over and over again.

My mother went with my father to Belgium ten years ago and visited the monastery where he was hidden. The people who rescued him came to Israel. I met them when I was five years old. They are listed at Yad Vashem among the "Righteous Gentiles." They have the medal and the certificate.[5]

While growing up, I lacked self-confidence. My father often told me that I resembled an "absent-minded professor," because I would lose things. I grew very tall, my arms were very long, and he would laugh at me. He may have laughed at my sisters, as well, but I was more sensitive, and it hurt me.

When I was a teenager, he and I went to return a video. He sent me into the store and he waited in the car. The manager scolded me for returning it late. I then realized that my father made me return it because he didn't want to face the manager. I became so angry as I understood that he couldn't take responsibility for his actions.

My parents have been separated for about six years. My father was unfaithful to my mother. I knew that something was wrong, but my mother didn't. I considered his conduct repulsive, but I kept it to myself. He saw another woman for ten years. People told my mother, but he continued to lie. He lived a life of lies, but was always excused for his behavior. I am disillusioned with his conduct; all my life I was told not to lie.

This woman with whom my father is having an affair is twenty years his junior. They work in the same place. She answers the telephone. She isn't a very educated person. My father is an electrician. He never wanted to improve himself in order to further his career, not in computer technology, not in French which, after all is part of his background. It was as though he feared he would fail. My mother made a career for herself after he left; she works with dyslexic patients.

Your father carries the typical "baggage" of a hidden child: the bursts of anger, the insecurities, the lies. Remember that in order to survive, he had to lie. When he came to Israel, he may have gotten into situations that he found uncomfortable. Then he most likely continued doing what he did all along in his childhood, that is, he lied. When you understand the causes for his behavior, you will be more able to forgive him.

I realize that when the Nazis took away my father's mother and sister, he was left by himself and that a kind stranger, although a gentile woman, took him in. Years later, after his surviving father returned from the camps and remarried, his stepmother was unkind to him. So, my father's father unburdened himself of my father by sending him to Israel.

Therefore your father must have a strong sense of abandonment. Was that sentiment transmitted to you in any way?

My mother overprotected me, but I was able to cope when I became an adult.

My poor relationship with my father engendered a lot of guilt in me. I have been blaming myself all along.

Was it fear of abandonment that prevented you from having relationships with men?

I had no relationship with a man until I was twenty-four. I think that it was due to my rapport with my father. I felt that I had no father in my life. At twenty-five, I had a serious relationship, and the man was a lot like my father. I realized the parallel after I broke up with him.

For example, when I was a young child, my mother would get up at night to bring my father some food because he suffered from ulcers. My boyfriend had no health problems, but he asked me almost every night, in the middle of the night, to bring him food because he couldn't sleep.

When I worked as a secretary, I met a family who invited me to come to Germany with them as an au pair. I stayed for one year. The father was Jewish, but not the mother. In the beginning, it was a good experience. Toward the end, I didn't get along with the father, but I handled the situation. At the time, I had anxieties. My biggest worry was that I might lose my mother, that she might die. I never feared for my father. After all, my mother was the one who protected me.

When you lived in Germany, did you feel that you were in the country of the perpetrators of the Shoah?

At times I did. I saw the portraits of the ancestors of the family with whom I was staying. I thought that I, too, could have had relatives and deep roots. Yet, I felt as though I had no past. However, I looked for reconciliation with the Germans.

My younger sister and I went to Austria with a group of Israelis-- I was twenty-four then. We were the only people of the second generation, the others were of the third generation. We went to Vienna and found the house where my father had lived. We found the cemetery where relatives lay buried. We traveled to the Tyrol. It was difficult for me when I saw old people. I wondered about their roles and attitudes toward Jews during the war. Somehow I was more comfortable in Germany. I felt hatred in Austria.

How do you compare yourself to people who don't have a parent with such a past?

I think that having a father such as mine made me a more sensitive person. When I met camp survivors at Amcha,[6] I started to cry. I feel that life is easier for people whose parents are not survivors, their burden is light, but I am different.

When I was in second grade, I had to tell a story. I knew that all the other parents were younger than mine, and I also knew that my father's story was different from the other fathers, because mine had been in a monastery. My mother didn't want me to write about my father's past, especially not about him being in a monastery. I have also always kept silent about my father's relative in Belgium who was with him in the monastery, and who converted to Christianity.

My mother is observant, but my father isn't. He never wore a *kipa.*[7] We lived in a religious community and I went to a religious school. I was ashamed to walk in the street with him, to bring my friends home because he wasn't observant. In a certain way I, too, had to hide. Yet, he does go to synagogue.

As I said before, I believe that your father is a very mixed up man; he has a confused identity. He still doesn't know who he is, he can't seem to find himself. He was psychologically damaged in his childhood. On the one hand he is religious, he goes to synagogue; on the other, he isn't, as is your mother. He wants to tell you about his past, yet he doesn't. Then he makes up stories, just as he did when he was hidden. He repeats the behavior of his childhood.

When his parents were deported he felt abandoned. He lost his mother, but his father came back from the death camp. However, he lost him again when his father remarried, because the new wife didn't want him. When your father came to Israel, he probably hid the fact that he was a child survivor because survivors were considered victims. At the time, Israeli society demanded a strong image of the individual and had no patience for victims. With your mother being observant, and your father not knowing if he is or isn't, this situation must have created friction between your parents. Furthermore, he was satisfied to be an electrician, but your mother wanted him to better himself. He didn't want to try, perhaps because so many things in his life had failed.

Of course, all of the above doesn't make it easier for you, but it helps you to understand. Once you are no longer angry with your father, you'll be a happier person. You shouldn't blame yourself. You must try to understand how very confused he is, how much he suffered. When we started this conversation you said, "He didn't suffer physically, he had enough to eat, he was never beaten." Many hidden children had these very same thoughts about themselves and dismissed their suffering. They thought they had no right to feel bad because they weren't in the camps. The fact is that there is no hierarchy in suffering. Your father was psychologically injured and he never had a proper childhood.

My husband always tells me that he is afraid that when my father will be no more, I will have big problems because I may feel very guilty. I should have a better relationship with him now.

For your own sake, you ought to establish such a relationship, make it as neutral and as pleasant as you can. If he is arrogant, you'll know why; try to disregard it. His arrogance serves as a protection against his insecurity. If you have specific questions, he may now be ready to answer them.

He didn't have the courage to tell your mother that they weren't suited to each other. Instead, he was untrue. That is a character flaw. It is a wonder that your sisters don't have any problems.

They may have different ones. He always thinks that others are at fault.

I want to be a good daughter to my mother, but my relationship with my father bothers me. My husband is most important to me. I also want children. I am not sure if I want an observant family. My husband isn't religious, yet his grandparents are. We need to work this out.

One night in Germany when I couldn't sleep, I thought about my father's mother after whom I was named. I thought that if she could see my relationship with my father, she would find it very painful.

What has our interview brought you?

You explained the reasons for my father's behavior toward me. Maybe I can be in contact just with his past, not with the way he is now.

I have a good relationship with my sisters. I am the only one whose rapport with him is bad. My sisters listen to his stories. I think that I took my mother's side, and maybe my older sister took my father's. My younger sister who is in the army now remained neutral; she is very diplomatic. All my sisters are married except for the youngest one.

Many of the children of hidden children have difficulties. Some of them are proud of their parents who overcame their problems, others resent them and blame them for their own insecurities.

Our discussion was very helpful to me; I have a clearer picture and a better understanding of my situation. Thank you.

NOTES:

1. Kibbutz. Cooperative farm.
2. Moshav. Multipurpose cooperative community.
3. Yad Vashem. See page 85 note 3.
4. *Amcha.* Hebrew word meaning "your people." Coalition for Jewish concern. Social organization.
5. Medal and Certificate. Awarded by Yad Vashem, the Holocaust Museum in Jerusalem, to people who saved Jews during the Holocaust.
6. *Amcha.* See note 4 above.
7. *Kipa.* Scull cap, worn by observant Jewish men.

OFRI

*I WAS VERY YOUNG
WHEN I FIRST HEARD ABOUT THE HOLOCAUST.
ONLY IN THE LAST FEW YEARS HAS IT AFFECTED ME.*

*Another child of a hidden child who came to see me at Kibbutz Alonim
was Ofri. From the start, she projected a very positive image of herself. She
seemed to be a well-balanced, cheerful individual. We met in the living
room area of the house we were staying in on the kibbutz, where I also met
with Tsilah, again on a hot June morning.*

I am well aware of my father's past, although there remain many
blank episodes that so far I haven't been able to fill-in. I try track-
ing them down as best I can.

My father was born in 1939 near Milan. His father was Jewish,
and was a partisan during the war. His mother was Christian. My
father's mother took my father, who was her third child, and his
two older brothers, to a village in the North of Italy to a family of
farmers. She felt that even though she was Christian, the children
might still be in danger of being persecuted. My father also had a
sister who was in a convent, and later she stayed with a Christian
woman.

My grandfather stayed in the forest. He would come to visit my
grandmother at night. My grandmother had younger children

with her, they were born during the war. One time when my grandfather came home, in 1944, one of the neighbors denounced him. He was deported and perished.

My father stayed in the village with the farmers for a while, but then he was moved--no one knows how, why, or when--to a place called San Bernadino. There was an institute there built by the Fascists for underprivileged children. This school was very well equipped and appointed. It even had a swimming pool.

When the war ended, people from Israel used the premises of the institute to assemble Jewish orphans from all over Europe, especially from Eastern Europe. They took care of them, they educated them, and eventually they sent them to Israel. No one knows how my father wound up in that institute. We know now that my grandmother's father went back to the village to get him, but he was no longer there.

My father was sent to Israel. He lived without an identity for twenty years--he never even knew how old he was. He was told that he was an orphan and that nobody knew who his parents were. It was known that he was from Italy, and that his last name was Cohen. When he came to Israel, he was called Arnaldo. However, no one knew his real name, so they gave him the name Danny, and they guessed his age.

My father wound up at Institute Onin, a children's home where half of the children were orphans and the rest came from under-privileged families. He remained there for about one year. Then a family who lived on a Kibbutz adopted him. He grew up on the Kibbutz where he was also educated.

One day, my father's family found him, after having looked for him for twenty years. My Christian grandmother knew nothing about Israel, she didn't know where it was, and she had no idea that he could be there. In 1970, the year I was born, a cousin of my grandfather who lived in Israel found my father. During the years when my father disappeared, very few children came from Italy. My father's cousin learned that a child named Cohen was sent to our Kibbutz. This cousin of my grandfather called the Kibbutz office and asked if a certain Arnaldo Cohen resided there. The people in the office promised to inquire further, but they didn't think there was any one there by that name. My father happened to be passing by the office when they said to him, "Danny, do you know anyone named Arnaldo Cohen?" My father didn't remember that this had been his name; he had been so young. Eventually, it was established that Arnaldo Cohen and Danny Cohen were one and the same person.

After this phone call, the family called from Italy. My father tried speaking to his mother, but she only spoke Italian and he only spoke Hebrew, so they couldn't communicate.

My father and I went to Italy together in 1991. We have a video-tape of the family meeting there. All the siblings had survived.

There is an organization of child survivors in the area from where my father came, but he has no connection with it. I suppose that the reason why this is so is because during those twenty years the mental climate in Israel was disdainful of survivors, they were considered victims. Israel rejected the notion--they considered themselves proud fighters, they repudiated all aspects of victim-hood. Therefore, the children who came to Israel continued to hide their past in order not to be considered weak. Consequently, all those years my father acted as though he had no connection to the Holocaust. After he found his family, he only spoke about the happy ending.

My father told me that when he came to Onin, the children's home in Israel, there were two dogs there. They were big and threatening, everyone was afraid of them. They were watchdogs that roamed freely during the night because of the many security problems. Often saboteurs tried to penetrate the Institute. My father made a special connection with these dogs, they came to his bedside at night. They were the only friends that he had dur-ing his time there. Nevertheless, he only spoke about positive feelings, never of any sense of loneliness.

During the last few years we established a memorial event on our Kibbutz. We light a candle for every person who is known to have been killed in the Holocaust, because so many of the six million have no one to memorialize them. This is done on all kibbutzim. My grandfather from my mother's side lost all of his family: seven brothers and sisters, cousins, nephews; they all perished in the death camps of Poland. Each member of our Kibbutz has relatives who died in the Holocaust. They light a candle and say their names. When this started, my father didn't participate, but then he saw that it was respected. I suppose that he thought about it, and a year later he asked me to light a candle to the memory of his father, because he had difficulty doing it. Now he does it himself every year, though his body language clearly shows his emotion. He does it very quickly, not wanting to betray the agitation that he has suppressed all these years. In this society, you had to grow up to become a warrior. Now the messages are very different, but my father, who developed in this former atmosphere, is still reluctant to speak. He isn't involved with any other hidden children. I don't know if he prefers not to be, we haven't discussed it.

Last year I found a beautiful book of survivors in our library. I gave it to my parents to read. In this book I found that there is an organization of survivors in Israel. I told my father that he ought to speak to them. A woman named Cohen from Italy is referred to in this book. I said to my father that she might be a relative. We know most of the relations in Italy, but the family was big, maybe we don't know of everybody. He didn't say that he didn't want to do it, he just ignored it. I haven't brought it up again.

I plan to make connection with this organization some day. Perhaps I can find someone who remembers him, perhaps there are pictures. I want to make a film of my father's life. I plan to investigate his story, but I first have to find time.

I have a suspicion that perhaps this identity that my father got twenty years after the war may not be his own. Maybe he is not Danny Cohen from Italy, maybe he is from Poland. Nobody really knows what happened. There is no mark on his body that his mother remembered. She wanted her child and he wanted a mother. We never spoke about it, but I think that maybe he is afraid that he may not even have any connection with the person thought to be him. The papers show no specific information that connects him to this family. There is a good chance that the family is really his, but it isn't one hundred percent certain.

He could find out with a DNA test.

He won't do it, it isn't that important. The family in Italy is very warm toward us; they are convinced that he is one of them, and he seems to be sure that he belongs to them. Even if it isn't true and he isn't really their son; he has his family now. He doesn't want to lose them again. His mother passed away eight years ago, but he has brothers and sisters.

If they have the same DNA, then he would know that they are indeed his siblings.

He isn't going to do that because life is stronger than any tragedy. He has gone on with his life, and it is good now. His specific knowledge of his genes is not that important. He has an Italian identity, and so do we.

My mother was born in Poland after the Holocaust. Her father was a Holocaust survivor. He escaped from the Warsaw ghetto when he was eighteen years old. He left his entire family there. He fled to Russia and returned to Poland after the war. For years he searched for his family, but found no one.

My mother's mother was a Russian Christian. My grandfather met her when he was there during the war. When they came to Israel, my mother, my grandmother, and my mother's brothers were all officially converted to Judaism.

I have five siblings, I am the second oldest. My oldest brother is also somewhat interested in my father's story, more so than the others. We don't really speak about it. I get all the information from my mother, but we children don't speak about it among ourselves.

When I was a teenager my father's story wasn't a secret, we all knew it. In the 1960s he was a known basketball player in Israel, he was well known all over the country. In 1970, when he found his family, the story was featured in all the Israeli newspapers. I wrote a paper about him in school.

At the end of my adolescence I began to connect things that happened in my own life with my father's life. For example, as far as I can remember, everyone considered me Italian, even though I was born in Israel. My mother is Polish, so I am half Polish. I was told that I looked Italian, and that I resembled my grandmother. In our living room there was a large decorative map of Italy. We ate a lot of tomato sauce with pasta, because it was Italian. For my father, everything Italian was good.

The family from Italy visited often when I was a child. They brought toys and pretty clothes. The house was full of things from Italy. I had a strong love for the Italian people, for the country. My father transmitted it to me.

I knew my father's story as a teenager, but my parents never made the connection to the Holocaust. When they spoke about it, they said, "during the war." They never referred to my father as a Holocaust survivor. So, I never thought of my father as a victim, only as a "poor child." He is a very strong man and to me he was a hero. He was a basketball player, he participated in all kinds of sports, he had been a soldier. He made us laugh. He would play with us--not the types of games that require a lot of thinking. He is generally a cheerful man, so I couldn't connect him to the Holocaust. To my mind, Holocaust survivors were broken, sad, and depressed; my father wasn't like that. For instance, when children didn't obey, he never said, "I wish that I had a mother and a father." When I complained about my mother, my father would say, "Family is the most precious gift. Even if you have friends, family will always stay with you." I internalized the idea profoundly.

I was very young when I first heard about the Holocaust. Here in Israel, we grew up with it. Only in the last few years has it affected me. I saw the film *Schindler's List*, and I cried. I also saw *The Garden of the Fizi Contini* when I was very young. In my twenties, I started to realize that my father is a Holocaust survivor and that I am "second generation." This made me very sensitive to everything that pertained to the subject. I am a sensitive person to begin with. Any suffering upsets me. I cannot tolerate mistreatment of animals. I have become even more impressionable within the last few years. I am easily moved to tears.

My father's past is a very important part of me. I don't feel burdened by it because I don't mind that this is an element of my life. It makes me sad, but I think that it also makes me a better person. I think that it makes me different from the people around me. When I was a child, the people on the Kibbutz said to me, "Oh, your father found his family!" It was a big story and everyone was so happy that it happened. This made me feel special.

I speculated about how old my father was when he was first taken to the Italian village, then to the institute for orphans, and later when he came to Israel. I compared him to my youngest brother, as well as my nephew--they were about the same age as my father was at the time. Then I thought, "Oh my God, he was so young!" I work with children and I think that they are very vulnerable. My father had to grow up overnight.

In many ways, however, I feel optimistic. This is a quality I inherited from my father. He is a very positive person, and a good father. He has his past, but he grew up to be such a good human being. Unfortunately, I could not communicate with my father's mother, since she only spoke Italian. I saw her many times and I got the impression that she was a calm individual. After my father found his family, my mother studied Italian; she speaks the language better than my father.

In your quest for your own identity, would you say that it is connected to your father's past, and your search for his particular past?

In part yes, but my identity has other components as well. My father grew up on the Kibbutz, therefore we share this cultural element. I must say that his past is much more part of me than my mother's past. She never speaks about it. Maybe it is because she has no need to do so. I asked her about it when I was a child. I think that she has no need to make her past part of her life now. My father wanted to build our identity as Italians. He feels very warm toward Italy, whereas my mother has the opposite feeling toward Poland.

My father's personality is very strong, his influence is powerful. We all feel Italian. Italians are very warm, sunny, welcoming, and they are fun to be with. Since my father didn't know his birthday, he never celebrated it. But for us children, our birthdays were big events. I think that this stems from the fact that as a child he was very sad because he could never celebrate his birthday.

Although my father is strong, I feel that I need to protect him. I won't let anyone criticize him, even my mother, although I know that she is right sometimes. My father is claustrophobic, he hates getting into elevators. At home we always have to have a window open. He told me that when he was in the army, he was asked to work on a submarine, he couldn't do it. My oldest brother has the same fear.

My siblings and I are very independent. Our father gave us a very strong feeling that he would be there for us should the need arise. He rarely gets angry--maybe now more than in the past, but not very much.

Since he was sent from one place to another during his childhood, do you think that he felt abandoned by his family?

He never speaks about it. I respect the fact that he may have had such feelings. My mother told me that my father has cousins here in Israel, but we have no connection with them. The first and only time they met, they made remarks about my father's mother implying that she hadn't been good to her children. As a result, we severed all contacts with them.

When I asked Ofri if she ever had any fear of abandonment, she laughed at the question, and replied that she hadn't.

Our kibbutz is atheist, however, in my family we observe *Brit Mila*,[1] *Bar Mitzvah*,[2] and in general we observe the holidays. We don't observe Shabbat, although my mother lights candles, but we don't have *challah*[3] and we don't have *Kiddush*.[4] For me, religion is an important issue. I took some courses about the Jewish religion which I found very interesting. We studied the Talmud and read the Mishna My father was circumcised. My parents had a Jewish wedding.

Did you always want to be Jewish?

I don't think about it, that is just who I am. However, I also know that part of my family is Christian. My grandmother wore a cross, it didn't bother me. When she came to Israel, my father took her to church.

I never experienced anti-Semitism, not in Italy, not in France, not in Switzerland, Sweden, or Denmark. My Israeli passport brought forth good reactions.

I am very much anchored in Israel. I am Israeli, and I want to live here. I am happy with who I am. I think that I am a good person, I am successful, my parents are proud of me. The latter is very important to me. I am very good in my work dealing with children. In terms of what occurred during the Holocaust, what happened to my father, all that history needs to be taught. People must know about it. I will carry this information with me and some day I'll tell my children.

My dream is to study in the U.S. for my Ph.D. However, I expect that it would be difficult to make this a reality. I would like to get married, but I am in no hurry. Right now I am busy with my career, but once I have children, they will be the most important part of my life. So I don't mind waiting even for another few years since I don't know if I'll be able to work once I have a family. Right now I am studying, traveling, having fun.

When my friend saw the article about your work, she read it to me because she knew how interested I am in the subject. I called Michal at Kibbutz Alonim and told her that I wanted to testify. I enjoyed talking with you about this very important part of my life.

NOTES:

1. *Brit Milah*. See page 105 note 2.
2. *Bar Mitzvah*. See page 105 note 1.
3. *Challah*. Special bread used in Jewish ritual.
4. *Kiddush*. Blessing recited over a cup of wine or grape juice to sanctify the Jewish Sabbath.

MURIEL

*MY MOTHER HAS TRANSMITTED TO ME
ALL THE SUFFERING THAT SHE HARBORED INSIDE HER,
AND WHICH IS STILL THERE.*

—~—

Paris was our next stop in our quest for witnesses.

We rented a friend's apartment in the 15th arrondissement. The following week we moved to a hotel in the heart of the city.

Muriel, came to see me at our apartment on a very warm June afternoon. She had been a teacher of English at a secondary school in the Paris suburbs. The students came mostly from families who emigrated from Algeria, Morocco, and Tunisia. She left her position because she found teaching there difficult due to the many disciplinary problems.

A good friend of mine knew her mother from continuing adult education classes they took together at the university. This was the connection that brought us together.

My mother is Jewish, but not my father. She is often critical of him for not understanding what happened to her during the war. He admits that he doesn't understand, and gets angry.

I know very little regarding my mother's past as a hidden child. I only know a few odds and ends, and I am incapable of questioning her.

Her parents came to France from Poland. My mother's older sister had been born there. The family lived in Paris for quite some time. My mother always suffered from the fact that her parents didn't speak French well. She was rejected and excluded in school because she had a foreign name. The fact that people mispronounced her name, which wasn't really difficult, distressed her. They did it on purpose. Therefore, she felt rejected starting from a very young age.

My mother's father was deported following the Vel d'Hiv ("Velodrome d'Hiver")[1] raid in June 1942. Then they heard rumors of a new raid, they learned that the French police were coming back. My mother's mother sent the three oldest children (and my mother was one of them) to the countryside to live with acquaintances of the family. She thought that she, herself, and the two very young children had nothing to fear. My mother, who was fifteen at the time, left with my aunt and my uncle. They hid near Grenoble and stayed with a gentile woman who worked at the city hall and clandestinely made false identity papers for them. My aunt has remained friends with her.

The three children who went to the countryside never saw any of their deported loved ones again. Indeed, the mother was arrested with the two little girls. None of them returned, nor did the father.

At the end of the war, my mother's sister, who was the oldest of the three siblings, was considered the head of the family. The relationship between my mother and her sister has always been difficult.

I was ignorant of the fact that because my mother was Jewish I was Jewish as well. I attended a public experimental elementary school. Everything was focused on the child's personality development rather than on acquired knowledge. The student body consisted of about three hundred to three hundred and fifty children. We all knew one another.

In my class, there was a boy who never came on Saturday. He also always wore a small beret. I would say to him, just like the others did, "Come on, take off that beret. Why do you always wear it?"--remarks to that effect. We didn't understand why he never came on Saturday. Thus, I remained totally ignorant of my origins. I don't remember precisely the time when I found out that my mother is Jewish. I know that I was in my teens. It is only recently that I started thinking about this boy in my class.

My father is an atheist, thus we celebrated Christmas as just another holiday when we exchanged gifts. Any information about my mother's origins was blocked. No doubt, my mother wanted to protect my younger brother and me, and probably herself as well. She released the information when I was about fourteen. I cannot remember how it all manifested itself; it came by bits and pieces. I recall coming into my parent's room on Sunday mornings and sometimes seeing my mother awaken suddenly and cry out, *Maman*!! I imagined that she had a nightmare. However, I never spoke with her about it, never. One day she must have told me that she had nightmares about what she had experienced.

Did you ever ask who your grandparents were and what had become of them?

No, I couldn't. My natural inclination prevents me from posing questions. I don't want to appear curious, nor do I want to seem ignorant. I knew that there was a secret there, and I didn't want to hurt her. I think that I could sense that it would cause her pain.

You must have asked yourself, "Where are my grandparents?"

At that time, children did not visit one another as they do today. I had friends in school, but I didn't see them in their private lives. Therefore, I never saw my friends' grandparents.

My paternal grandparents lived in the South of France, in Toulon. I seldom saw them. However, I felt immense joy when we got together.

Didn't you wonder where was this ""Maman" that your mother cried out for when she woke up?

I can't remember how I learned about it. I didn't question my mother before coming to see you. I thought that if I had, my testimony wouldn't be genuine. She wanted me to meet you. She also asked my brother, who is five years younger. He wasn't interested.

When she asked me I said yes at once. My brother, who is somewhat complicated said, "I want to know what will be done with my remarks." The big difference between my brother and me is that I feel totally Jewish, and he not at all. That is also the reason why he didn't want to testify.

Of course, the fact that one feels kinship with the Jewish people, even in a secular fashion, may encourage an individual to testify. However, regardless of whether one considers oneself Jewish, the subject of this study is the transmission of the Jewish parents' experience to the children.

My brother married a gentile girl. My first husband's father was Jewish. My oldest daughter, whose father is my first husband, feels completely Jewish. My second daughter does too, of course.

Thus, I found out that my mother is Jewish, and that consequently I am, too. Later, my mother started taking courses since she had had no opportunity to study due to the events in her early youth during the German occupation. I believe that one course concerned the history of the Jewish religion.

When I was sixteen or seventeen, she started to speak. By then she was completely obsessed by the subject, which would always come up in conversation. Whatever the theme of the discussion, she always managed to return to the same topic. She could no longer abandon the matter.

However, she never attended any conferences of Hidden Children, or gatherings of Child Survivors of the Holocaust. I believe that she lacked the courage to do so. She isn't connected to any organization.

Did you ever question your Father?

No. I cannot speak to him. It doesn't come out.

My mother has transmitted to me all the suffering that she harbored inside her, which is still there. That is the reason why I am so Jewish, this pain that I feel. I am so afraid of my mother suffering, so worried that her eyes may fill with tears, or whatever. Therefore, I avoid the subject. I would be incapable of visiting a concentration camp. I hope that my mother never does because that would demolish her completely.

Recently, she had to write a letter in order to obtain a pension as compensation for her losses during the war. She kept saying, "I can't do it, I can't bring myself to do it. Oh this is such a worry, I am in a terrible state." I told her, "Look, if you want me to, I'll write the letter, I'll make that request for you." Yet she replied, "No, no, I can do it, it is done already, it is only a printed form that had to be filled out."

Well, I got some information through another aunt, the wife of my mother's brother. She, too, is Jewish. She lost everyone in her family. The two sisters-in-law are not on speaking terms. I blame my mother, under the circumstances. Can you imagine that two people who have suffered so could quarrel?

Yes, I can very well envision such a quarrel. Holocaust survivors are like everyone else. From time to time they may squabble and be narrow-minded, just like the rest of the population.

I imagine so. In any case, my aunt gave me the information as to what needed to be done concerning this mail. She is very active and knowledgeable in many subjects. She belongs to an organization called "Jewish Memory." She is well informed on current events.

My aunt told me what needed to be done. I followed her directions and then I advised my mother of the fact that I had taken care of the matter. She asked me, "How did you know what to do?" So, I had to lie, because they were angry with one another. Therefore, I invented some explanation or other.

As soon as I gave her the letter that I wrote, she told me that she had already done it herself. However, what she had written was not clear, it was too involved and complicated. She then started to cry. I cannot stand seeing her cry, so I said to her, "You did it well, send the whole thing off." Then I abandoned the subject. It hurts me as much as it hurts her. That isn't normal, because I had a happy childhood, I didn't experience the war. Even my husband, who was born in Algeria, endured the war *there*. He saw cadavers when he was a child. I never knew any of that, therefore I shouldn't feel such suffering.

I think that it is perfectly normal since you empathize with your mother. There are many possibilities why you are burdened by your mother's past.

She says that someday she will tell it all to her granddaughters.

People don't understand when I say that I am Jewish, but that I don't believe in God. I had a conversation with a friend who is quite a bit younger than I. He is a very pious practicing Sephardic Jew. He told me that he could not understand such a point of view.

Yes, but then he never experienced the distress that you feel.

My mother is very severe with people who haven't suffered. That is why she rejects the Sephardic Jews. True, my husband is Sephardic, too, since he was born in Algeria. My in-laws are not very enlightened. They have only learned recently what was done to the Jews of Europe.

That is very surprising to me, even for people who are not well informed. You say that you don't think that it is normal to be so burdened with the weight of your mother's past. I can tell you that it is very normal. Certain people feel it very keenly, others don't. Many daughters identify with their mother, they have close and strong relationships. However, it seems to me that you are Jewish because the Jews have suffered. It is with the Holocaust that you identify your Judaism?

My mother-in-law celebrates the Jewish holidays, and this delights me. These celebrations are very important to my daughters. I don't do it in my house because my mother never did. I don't even know the dates of the festivals. How could I celebrate these events if I don't believe in God? For people who have never done this, whatever is religious makes them smile a bit. I don't fast on *Yom Kippur*[2] since it doesn't represent anything for me. However, my daughters do fast. They don't know exactly why. It pleases their paternal grandmother. When my mother found out, she said, "After all, why not." My father is very intolerant, he doesn't understand. His motto is atheism, first and foremost. Again, as far as I am concerned, I find the festivals too connected with religion.

When you were dating, did you go out with non-Jews?

I wasn't concerned whether they were Jewish. When I was twenty-two, I married my first husband, who was Jewish through his father. Yet, later it became important to me to marry a Jewish man, I don't know why. I told myself that it was better for me.

My oldest daughter only dates Jewish boys. Not so the younger one, who is seventeen. I am very open, honest, and direct with my daughters, I believe it is very important. We discuss every subject.

Were your parents happy in their marriage?

Yes, they have many tastes in common. Yet they quarreled a lot about banal and silly reasons. Sometimes they bickered about politics. My mother always had to make a remark about a politician who had been clumsy, or about some person who had said something else that irritated her.

For instance, she went to a ceremony at City Hall where someone made an allusion about people who had died in the Holocaust but who weren't Jewish. This didn't please my mother, she felt that the Holocaust had to be treated separately and differently. This sort of subject is one my mother brings up endlessly. Ultimately, it exasperates me, but I say nothing. I have had conflicts with my mother, but, I am ready for all the compromises in order to avoid such conflicts.

I understand that it was difficult for my mother to speak about her suffering. At first there was only silence, then constant discussions followed on the subject. She has calmed down these days.

We frequently go out together--she lives near us. I would like to say to her, "Mother tell me." I know that she would start crying. Again, I cannot stand to see her cry. Perhaps I will try, some afternoon, going out with her by myself, or with my daughters.

It seems to me that it would be better if she were alone with you. No doubt, she would like to express herself, but she doesn't want to make you cry, either. Therefore, you both suffer; it is a vicious circle.

I would prefer for her to talk, but when she does, it is always aggressively. She always has something reproachful to say. The fact that she has been so marked by her past has made her a bit paranoid. My aunt is not that way. I think that with my mother it has become excessive, but I don't reproach her. For the people close to her it is often difficult. I understand why my father has often had enough.

I have never said to my mother that I suffer like her. I don't think that she knows. Everyone else who surrounds me does, my husband knows. Maybe my mother does, too.

Did your mother get angry easily?

She often got angry with me at the start of my adolescence. Maybe I was intolerable. Personally, I think that I was too good. I remember a time when she would yell at me, and I didn't think that I had done anything bad. She would get angry less often with my brother. After some time she calmed down.

The silence and feeling of secrecy, of uneasiness, must have influenced your childhood and your adolescence. You knew that there was a secret, but you didn't dare to ask any questions.

Perhaps it acted on my nature, causing me to have this disposition that I do of not daring to question.

When I was a child, my mother's sister had two daughters; she lost a son. Then she acquired another daughter. When I was ten I understood that this third daughter was adopted; she was a year older than her oldest daughter. My aunt never spoke of her parents.

My mother never played with me when I was small; in any case, she played very little. I have no memories of her telling me stories. We were seldom together because she worked long hours. When my father was away, we played a little in the evening. I must have been very young, because my brother wasn't born yet. Sometimes she walked me to school and we would sing walking songs on the way.

Where would you go if things were bad in France?

I have never asked myself that question. I went on vacation on Maurice Island, in the Indian Ocean, east of Madagascar. All the different communities on that island live in relative harmony. Maybe I would go there.

What does Israel mean to you?

It is a country of which I am very critical for what I consider to be racism between the Sephardic and the Ashkenazi Jews. Also, this hatred against the Arabs is something that I cannot integrate. However, I understand that the country needs to defend itself.

What about France, are you anchored here?

It is my country, I was born here, it is my nationality, but no more than that. I like the current sentiment of modernization, to be a citizen of everywhere a bit. Yes, I consider myself European, but no more than that either.

I went to Germany and met the most charming people. The man was of my generation. As I looked at his very Aryan features I couldn't stop asking myself what his father had experienced. Neither my husband nor I asked him any questions. I see no obstacles of their being in the European community. I think that this second generation of Germans has enormous guilt feelings.

Have you ever been the victim of anti-Semitism?

Not in school, not at the university, nor in my professional life. Not at all. I have intimate friends who are not Jews. I mention very quickly, and easily that I am Jewish. I may have heard some anti-Semitic remarks, but they were never directed at me. They were stupid reflections rather than anti-Semitic. The people who surround me, even those who only know me slightly, know that I am fiercely antiracist.

Do you believe that your mother suffers from feelings of abandonment?

Yes, I do.

Have you experienced such fears?

No, not fear of abandonment, but deep feelings of guilt. I constantly have the feeling of being battered. I feel guilt toward everyone who is close to me. I often asked myself whether I was capable of having had a happy childhood when my mother's was so unhappy. For a time, I consulted two psychologists, but they didn't help me. The process didn't move fast enough for me. I think that I feel guilty for having had a happy childhood, a happy adolescence, and a happy adulthood.

Have you ever felt that your mother needed protection?

No, I never have. She always was able to rely on herself.

Do you have confidence in yourself?

No. I never have, and I still don't. I believe that this stems from my education and from my relationship with my mother. It may also come from the time when she wouldn't speak about her past.

I had enough independence; I knew that she would be there for me if I needed her. My father was the strict one, he laid down the rules. I was never late coming home. If I was, I wouldn't be able to go out the following week.

I assumed my full independence when I became an adult. I was forced to do so due to the fact that my husband was often away on trips.

How is your mother's relationship with your daughters?

It is excellent. I believe that she told them already that some day she would tell them all about her past. My brother has two little girls, the oldest is six. I am sure that she knows nothing about her grandmother, absolutely nothing.

My children are well informed. My husband and I took them to see the film "Life is beautiful." I couldn't sit still, I didn't stop railing against it, and I influenced them completely. I couldn't stand this film, I think it is a disgrace. I told my mother, "Above all, don't see it." Even among the current generation, they think that people were joking in the death camps. I was in such a state, I shouldn't have reacted in that way.

Are you glad to be Jewish?

I have never asked myself that question. I have never wanted to be anything else. I think that being Jewish made me sensitive toward my fellow human beings.

The people who are most important to me are my mother, my husband, and my daughters. I now realize that for my own well being, as well as for my mother's, the two of us have to have a very frank discussion soon. I believe that my mother wants to talk.

Muriel informed me consequently that she and her mother had a very productive discussion. This resulted in good feelings for both of them. It made her mother happy.

NOTES:

1. Vel d'Hiv raid. Abbreviation for "Velodrome d'Hiver," raid by Vichy French police on July 16, 1942. Approximately 9,000 Jewish adults and 4,000 children were kept in this sports arena, and then deported.
2. Yom Kippur. Day of Atonement. Jewish holiday observed over twenty-four hours with fasting and prayer

CLARA

*I TRY TO FIND HOW THIS ANGUISH REACHED ME,
THIS BURDEN THAT I CARRIED DURING A GREAT PART
OF MY LIFE.*

Clara was a friend of one of my witnesses who told her about my project. Both of her parents had been hidden in France. She contacted me because she was very interested in the topic. We arranged to meet at my hotel, where we found a quiet spot in the lobby.

Clara was forty-five, and vibrant. Paris was her home, and her work dealt with theater sets and props. She referred to herself as a bit artistic, and somewhat of an itinerant.

Clara was nervous; during our discussion she consumed several bottles of Badoît water that we ordered from the hotel.

My parents never wanted to speak of their experience. All they said was, "We were hiding at such and such an age." Other than some facts they shared, meaningful details always remained obscure.

I never asked many questions. I didn't realize what lay underneath the surface. I called them this morning to ask for information.

Were your parents interested in our meeting?

They weren't against it, but there was something lifeless in their answers. As far as they are concerned, knowing isn't forbidden. However, something is taboo, and remains obscure.

My mother was hidden at age seven with her younger sister, who was two. From 1942 to 1944, they lived with a Gentile couple southeast of Paris in an area called Nièvre. When I asked my mother if she had other little girls with whom to play she replied, "I don't want to remember any of that, it hurts too much."

My father is ill now, so I didn't insist, but I asked him how old he was when he was hidden. He told me, "July 16, 1942." But that isn't correct, that is the date his mother was arrested and deported when the French militia, doing the dirty work for the Germans, raided Jewish homes. They took the people to the "Vel d'Hiv"[1] (Velodrome d'Hiver,) a bicycle sports arena. From there, they transported them to the assembly camp at Drancy, near Paris.[2]

When my father's mother was taken, she was in the street with her children: my father, his younger brother, and his little sister. The Germans wanted to take the children, too, but a neighbor who happened by asked for the children, she said that she would take care of them. The neighbor left with the children, and the mother left with the Germans. Maybe they were from the French militia and not Germans, I don't know exactly. She was never heard of again, other than perhaps a letter from the camp in Drancy.

My father was hidden when he was twelve and thirteen with his brother, who was two years younger. They hid in Montsauché, also in the Nièvre area.

My mother's father was taken to the camp in Drancy. But my mother's mother was employed by an organization called "UJIF,"*Union des Juifs de France"* (Union of Jews of France,) and it is thanks to her job that she was able to get her husband out of Drancy. My grandmother worked in an orphanage. I was told that she took care of children whose parents had been deported and who were French Jews.

I informed Clara of what I knew about the UJIF and the fact that the people who worked for this agency were protected from Nazi persecution for a while. This organization was an intermediary between the Nazis and the Jewish Community. She was very disturbed by this information.

Although I know little about my father's father, I believe that he wasn't in Paris. I think I was told that he had left for the *"Zone Libre,"*[3] the part of France that was governed by Pétain with the capital in Vichy. I can't tell you for certain because my father became completely estranged from his family, turning rather toward my mother's. He took my mother's mother as his own. He built for himself a new family, with my grandmother at the center. My father's father married again. My father never spoke of what had happened. We saw little of my father's father

My mother's parents are of Greek extraction. Their ancestors fled Greece at the time of the Inquisition. They spoke Ladino.[4] Every year there is a Judeo-Spanish celebration. At one of these celebrations there was a stand for the hidden children. I took some of the literature and went to show it to my parents. They weren't interested.

I believe that I was sixteen when I first heard about the Holocaust. My mother showed me photographs of the camps. That is what I remember as the first time. I must have heard of it before, I can't say for sure. I remember this episode because it dealt with my family. I took it to be my history because my mother showed me pictures. It is this incident that marked me.

However, my mother didn't explain that my grandmother disappeared in the camps. It was as if she never existed. I never asked because one cannot ask about someone who doesn't exist.

In my parent's house there is a large frame containing photographs of many family members, even of some distant relatives, but there wasn't one picture of my grandmother. This is stupefying! Some years ago I said that we should add a picture of my father's mother. I didn't dare to say "my grandmother's picture," because no one ever speaks of her, she is so terribly blacked out. Following my request, they added her picture. Yet, on the other hand, they named me after her. At the time her name was Chaya, meaning "life." They translated it to Clara. She doesn't exist, but at the same time I am her incarnation.

I think that my father carries his mother in his heart, which was broken by her loss. Her presence is too strong for him, one can sense it. My father has a sharp sensitivity. He suffers, he is anguished, he is very nervous. To my mind, all of this is due to his story. When my father was twelve and thirteen, he must have thought of himself a man, and most likely felt guilty for not having done anything in regard to his mother.

Children of hidden children realize that their parents are fragile and they want to protect them. Of course, my father wants to protect me as well. But beyond that, I think that one asks no questions on a matter that is obliterated.

Yet her picture is there.

Yes. However, everything was done so that I would believe that she didn't exist. At the time, I was a child who couldn't reason, who wanted to act according to her parents' wishes. If the parents don't want to discuss it, so be it. One cannot, at age three or four, oppose one's parents.

Perhaps you couldn't ask at age three or four, but at twelve or thirteen?

In my adolescence, I had so many problems, as most teenagers have. I sensed the taboo, therefore I couldn't ask any questions. It was my parents' secret world that didn't translate into words, but into emotions by their silence.

My maternal grandmother spoke the most often about the Holocaust. She lived through it as an adult. Perhaps it was less difficult than experiencing it as a child. My grandfather didn't speak of it, he spoke very little at all.

My mother had three sisters. One who was two at the time she was hidden with her. I was told that she was treated better than my mother because she was a baby. When the couple had their own child, they treated my mother's sister the same as my mother. My grandmother kept the youngest with her, and I don't know where the oldest went. You can see that I wasn't told very much. I learned from my mother that she had to look after the cow when the animal was about to have a calf. But I never knew any of this when I was a young girl, never.

My father never spoke of the family who hid him, he just said that his life was difficult. At one point, he had to kill a dog, and the peasants were harsh with him. He never mentioned that when he was hidden he didn't know where his parents were.

My mother never told me what her life was like when she was hidden with the French couple. I simply heard the family speak of it occasionally. A few years ago, I started questioning her. I imagined her like "Cosette," in Victor Hugo's *Les Misérables*, the little girl carrying two buckets. In fact, this is much the way her life had been. This morning she said to me on the phone that the people who hid her forgot to feed her, that she ate with the pigs, that she fetched water in buckets. She was frightened, insecure, and she feared the world. I wonder how one can reconstruct oneself after such experiences. She always repeated that she didn't want to remember, because it was too painful.

Although my parents are not practicing Jews, they have never denied who they are. They always say that they are proud to be Jewish. When I think of their childhood, I wonder how children could have had any self-respect when they saw that Jews were persecuted. How does one keep one's human dignity when one hears everywhere that Jews smell bad, that Jews are flunkies, etc.? How does one manage to construct oneself? How can one oppose the words of adults? How could my mother, who was so young, have kept her self-esteem?

I try to find how this anguish reached me, this burden that I carried during a great part of my life. I suffer from insomnia, I take medication, and I am plagued by anguish. As a small child I had frequent nightmares. Apparently, I didn't let my mother sleep at night, I wouldn't stop crying. I was told that I was bad. I was as frightened of my father's voice as of my nightmares. For years I couldn't fall asleep unless my mother told me that I wouldn't have any dreams, nor would I have nightmares. My childhood was constantly filled with distress.

My father planned a scheme to cast off his wife, my mother, in everyday life. I had his mother's name and I was a very intelligent child. Thus, my father put all his hopes on his little girl, who was supposed to make up for what he had lost. He got very attached to me, to the point where we seemed a couple, and my mother was rejected. I think that my mother was aware of it. Our relationship was very bad.

Could it be that your mother reproaches you for this complicity with your father?

It is all kept in silence. I discovered not too long ago that there was a matter of a double lie. I thought for a long time that I had sided with my father. This wasn't so, because down deep I took my mother's side. In everyday life, I sided with my father, but I suffered for my mother, she represented for me little Cosette. Therefore, I most likely searched my conscience, and I must have felt terribly guilty for doing this to my mother, yet I didn't realize it.

We never had any discussion about this. I made up with my mother a while ago because my father is very ill.

My father leads a double life. He is a man of great generosity, with a big heart, who can be very tactful. At the same time, he can be a tyrant, extremely nervous and violent.

He would tell me, "I am going to kill you, stop that!!" This was because I would resist him, mainly in my adolescence. I answered back, I was fresh, and he threatened me. He hit me. He would rip off his belt. I had black and blue marks. I started to defend myself. I insulted him, I called him a coward, a beast who would hit someone smaller than himself. But it was a passionate relationship in the first degree--one of great violence.

Did your mother try to intervene?

I think that she must have--anyhow a little bit. But my father locked himself in with me in my room. I remember the violence, but I don't remember that he really hurt me.

My mother rarely got angry. My grandmother tried to calm it all, to do good. She raised me when my parents were involved in business, when they traveled. I was with my grandmother several months during the year. With her, my childhood was normal. She was generous, but she was worried.

Did your parents play with you?

All I know is that I wasn't allowed to cry. I never played with my father. I think that my mother told me stories, but did she play with me? I don't remember. Even in terms of touching, I find a large void. I don't remember having been cradled and rocked. My grandmother most probably held me a lot. In terms of my parents, I only feel emptiness.

My mother had a serious nervous breakdown when I was an adolescent. I was blamed for her illness, and told that her condition resulted from when I was very young and wouldn't let her sleep. But when I speak about it, they say, "But we never said that to you." I am sure that I heard it.

I was very obstinate as an adolescent. My mother's illness nearly killed her, and I was blamed for that, too, because I was rebellious. My mother had suffered since childhood. If she could only have known that that's what plagued her and made her sick, not I.

I enjoyed no independence. My father would bar the door, and I would scream. I had nervous fits, I wanted to leave. I don't know at what age I was allowed to go out, all I know is that it was late compared to my girlfriends. I had a very independent nature. I am the opposite of what they were trying to do with me, I am not at all conventional. This is another matter, because my parents are extremely conventional. I think that a lot of Jews were that way because to be different was dangerous. Thus I, someone of a very different nature, had my personality stifled.

I have the impression that in my immediate family people have great trouble having children. I have no children. My sister who is thirty-four shares her life with a man, but she has no children. One of my two cousins had a child at thirty-eight or thirty-nine, the other is forty and has none. One cousin who went to live in Israel has two children.

I wanted no children, I was too uncomfortable with myself, and I had too many anxieties. I had a big job ahead of me figuring it all out. Also, I wasn't about to be part of a couple because I was unsteady, I had too much work regarding myself, so that having a child, . . . it was all too complex.

I have a sister who is nine years younger than I. She is generally interested in Judaism. I don't think that she is interested in "hidden children." I believe that she didn't suffer the way I did. It was different for her; my father, who was totally concerned with me, neglected her. No doubt, this was painful for her, but she was very close to my mother.

Following violent inner turmoil, I underwent three psychoanalyses. At the same time, I started an organization called "Association of Mistreated Children." But at the time, I wasn't aware at what point I was personally involved. This came to the fore only after having spoken of my relationship with my parents during my analysis. However, we didn't speak very much about hidden children; psychologists didn't consider this matter of great importance. Perhaps the situation has changed now, because I did this fifteen years ago when I was thirty. It is amazing that they didn't think that there could be a link with this matter, and this particular psychologist was Jewish.

Thus, I started this agency not knowing that my mother had been mistreated. I discovered it later, as well as the fact that I hadn't been well treated, either. But I believe that I mostly lived my mother's experience. This suffering was transmitted to me involuntarily. I wonder if perhaps my little girl mother was raped; I don't know how far it went. I have had so many nightmares.

My grandmother died about ten years ago. I don't think that she could have enlightened me on the subject. The taboo is key in this entire story, as far as I am concerned.

In your opinion, your parents think that if you don't talk about a problem it will disappear. Many people refuse to speak because they feel that as soon as they do, the pain intensifies.

But it is transmitted to the next generation. If I had had a child during this earlier period that I spoke of, before I did all this psychological work regarding myself, I would have transmitted it, too.

Do you think now that your mother had a breakdown because you were troublesome?

Now I know that there were two principal reasons: one was my father's harshness, he was very macho. It's true, I didn't help things, either. The second reason was my mother's hurt in terms of my behavior. I sided with my father, and so I abandoned my mother. But that wasn't really so, because deep down I am sure that it was my mother who was important to me. I never spoke with my mother about the subject. I am certain that I hurt her deeply. Yet, I am not the main character in all of this. Now I have reached a certain level of maturity and we have started to get along well.

I think that I am similar to my father. I suspect that he transmitted his nature to me. When I wasn't allowed to go out, I was beside myself. My father was a despot. Furthermore, he could make a scene over trivial things. In the outside world, he is the opposite. Deep inside he is the opposite too; he is generous; he looks after the whole family, he lends his support financially. He is a two-faceted man, and I suffered greatly. He didn't want me to leave home, he wanted me for himself.

Did your mother undergo analysis too?

Not at all. My parents don't want to hear of it. They believe that they were model parents. As far as they are concerned, I had no reason to be disagreeable; I had the best parents in the word. It was my fault entirely, I was the ugly one.

My father wanted especially that I work hard in school, that I be the best in my class. And when I was, it was never good enough. Never was I told, "That's very good my darling." Never. Maybe from my mother, I can't remember. I got beaten when it wasn't good.

My parents couldn't accept my being so different from them; they wanted me to be as "normal" as possible. It was most striking in terms of clothing. Until puberty, I always wore the same red and navy blue dress, white socks, little shoes, and a small bow in my hair. I sensed from the adults that as children they needed to hide, they needed to be unnoticed. My parents feared my being different. But at the same time, they wanted me to be the best student. I had the right to be different there. Therefore, I had a difficult journey to travel in order to know who I was, and what I wanted. It was terrible for me to find myself.

There are so many things I need to say. Among my anxieties there is of course, culpability, but there are most of all threats everywhere in the world: the darkness of night, the houses, everything is threatening. I have improved a lot, but I cannot go to sleep without medication or I have terrible nightmares. I had frequent headaches. I often felt like weeping, but I had no right to do so. I couldn't go out mornings, because I felt too wounded, I was all on edge; of course none of these were rational fears.

Now I can go out but I am still prone to migraines which remind me of anxieties where everything becomes aggressive: any kind of odor, any kind of light--everything is hostile. My migraines come to tell me something that I haven't yet understood. As a matter of fact, I have a migraine now.

Clara went looking in her purse for some tablets, which she nervously unwrapped and swallowed with still some more Badoît.

My rapport with my sister is somewhat cool. She has fulfilled my father's dream. My father wanted us to be physicists, he had hoped to have sons rather than daughters. Well, my sister is a professor of physics. On the other hand, one day my mother mentioned that she would have liked to be an artist. Perhaps I am the one who has fulfilled my mother's dream. She certainly has an artistic nature that has been totally stifled.

I have no religious affiliation. I consider myself a human being; I try to be as good a person as I can. As far as I am concerned, all humans are equal. It would make no difference to me if the person with whom I might share my life weren't Jewish. Love is what matters, the rest is unimportant. If he weren't Jewish, he would bring me the security that I lack.

But, do you think that it is important to speak about what happened to the Jewish People during World War II?

Certainly, I think that your work is tremendous. I think that I have been waiting for you to come and question me. I have the need that all my pain be recognized in light of the fact that I was a child of hidden children. Now I will be a lot more myself.

My rapport with men is influenced by my experience with my father. I always felt that I needed to lie in order to be believed. I became conscious of it not too long ago. I said to myself, "What is this, why am I doing this!" I think that one explanation could be the recollection of the little girl facing daddy, the child who was going to be punished because she wanted to assert herself. What is worse is that such behavior is strictly contrary to my character. I am an honest and frank individual.

I often think that the truth won't suffice, people will not believe me, that I have to add something. When I was young, I was hit when I lied--mostly for childish lies of no significance whatsoever. I had done something foolish and I didn't want to be punished, so I said that I hadn't done it. The result was that heavens came crashing down on me.

My mother intervened sometimes, she put herself between my father and me. But I had rejected her, my poor mother who had suffered so greatly.

The wonder is that all these shadows became marvels of my inner life, of my comprehension of the world, and in my artistic life I am starting to be creative. As yet I haven't expressed everything. I certainly know these shadows very well, it was difficult to turn them into light. When I was seventeen or eighteen, everything came crashing down. I had no more sense of value, I didn't know what was true, what was false, what was worth doing. Later, I realized that tolerance had worth, that one should never be intolerant toward others. Of course, it took me years before I could succeed in this endeavor, and I am starting to get there. I am under the impression that as I advance in life, I transform the former pain into creativity; it's a process, a road that I have undertaken. I have blossomed, I am happy to be alive. I wouldn't have said so three years ago.

What are your thoughts about being French?

I am a citizen of the world, but I am attached to French culture. Israel is not a country that appeals to me. I am attracted by Italy. My work deals with opera, *Comedia del Arte*. I think that it is important for people like me to find lightness in life. I am tired of Paris, I would like to live in the south where there is lots of sunshine.

After recovering from her nervous break down, my mother resumed her life. Now she no longer lets herself be pushed around. She defends herself against my father's macho ways.

My father has cancer. The doctors told my sister and me that he had two months left to live. However, a miracle happened with him: he was supposed to have already died, but his cancer has regressed sixty percent. He took trips to Egypt and to Israel.

He and I have made up; I try to be nice to him. Of course, I don't take any abuse anymore.

Formerly, you weren't able to speak of your past, of your mother, of your father, or of the grandmother of whom no one spoke. Nevertheless, you overcame all of the secrets and taboos. Are you still searching?

I have undergone great hardships and have overcome them. I am marked for life by the fact that I need medication. I must take it at night in order to be able to sleep. Yet next to my father's illness, everything seems insignificant.

I remain someone who struggles for more justice, who still searches for herself, someone who wants to share happiness. I believe that we are here to be profoundly happy. I know that this earth could be like paradise, a place to which we should return.

Isn't it ironic, I have been unhappy for such a long time, and I speak to you of paradise.

NOTES:

1. Vel d'Hiv. See page 143 note 1.
2. Drancy. See page 85 note 2.
3. Zone Libre. Free Zone. See page 85 note 1.
4. Ladino. Judeo-Spanish spoken among Sephardic Jews.

MICHÈLE

*THERE WERE TIMES WHEN I FELT BURDENED;
I NO LONGER WANTED TO HEAR ABOUT IT.
I WISHED THAT MY MOTHER WOULD
STOP LIVING IN THE PAST.*

A close friend recommended that I get in touch with Michèle. I contacted her via email from the United States. We agreed that I would phone her when I got to Paris. Our interview took place in her home.

I am forty-three years old, I am married and we have a son who is eight. I work as an executive in customer service for a telephone company.

My mother's parents immigrated to Belgium from Poland, they lived in Brussels when my mother was born. The war broke out when my mother was seven years old. She was in hiding for about three years, starting at age ten. She told me that she hid in various places because they were denounced and had to move several times. She remembers best the time she stayed at a farm on the French border with a family, which was the place she remained the longest.

What would you say has been transmitted to you from your mother's experience?

A lot of unspoken transmission was made of images and feelings of terror, of anguish, of fears of the unknown, and of separation from parents. All these feelings have saturated my childhood, my adolescence, and even my adulthood. They date back so far that I cannot even remember when they began. I have always known them. I cannot say at what age the images became prominent, but I was extremely young.

The topic was often the subject of conversation; I sometimes asked questions. Mother gave details about her experience, she explained how and what she felt. She described the fear, the wretchedness of her existence, and the filth. When I questioned her, she answered willingly. She always needed to give voice to her memories, she needed to share them.

The event that marked me most was when we visited the family that had harbored her in the countryside. When we lived in the United States, we often went to Europe. Each time my mother would go to see them. Thus it was there that I could visualize the place were it all happened. She showed me the garden that she crossed when she ran alone in the night when Germans came around. She showed me the church where she went to hide. She would be awakened and told: "Get up quickly and run to hide in the church." Previously, it had been like a film for me, but when I saw the place, I became conscious of the reality.

Now that I have a child, I am more sensitive to this anguish, to this fear. When I was small I had some difficulty internalizing this information, I could make no analysis. Now that I am a mother I can imagine the distress of a parent who has to separate from her child. I can picture the pain of the child separated from her parents in a context so completely chaotic and terrifying.

There were never any secrets about my mother's past. Frankly, I would say that almost too much was said. She needed to share with us what she had lived through, the difficulty that she had experienced. My mother expressed this without end, and a great deal of this anguish was transmitted to us. There were times when I felt burdened, I no longer wanted to hear about it. I wished that that my mother would stop living in the past.

Your father is American. Didn't he protect you when your mother's need for sharing became burdensome to you?

No. When I told my father that I thought that my mother was ill, he replied that he didn't think so, because when they were first married, my mother would wake up at night screaming. He said, "If you had seen her when I met her, you would agree that it was then that she was ill."

My parents were twenty-five at my birth, they were twenty-nine or thirty when my brother was born. When we lived in the United States my father was in a difficult professional situation. He was often at home, but participated little in our education. My mother was very involved in our lives.

Has she had medical treatments?

Bad ones. The people weren't competent. My mother is obsessed by medicine, but only "soft," homeopathic, medicine—very "bio," never psychotherapeutic. **(Adding with a bitter laughter)** I am the one who takes these treatments, I started six months ago.

This older generation believed that such care was for demented people

Yes, that is what my mother believes. Incontestably, the need for my treatments is the result of my childhood.

Did your mother get angry easily?

Yes, my mother suffers from pathological nervousness. She jumps from her seat when one closes a door. When the phone rings, she worries, "Who could that be?" In spite of all the love I have for her, in spite of all the allowances that my brother and I, and my father have made, there comes a time when one has to protect oneself. Not doing so would engender perverse effects on our relationship with others, our attitudes with our life's partner, as well as our behavior as a parent. One must distance oneself from that influence. My mother grew up speaking Yiddish with her parents. She learned to speak French from a neighbor who looked after her while her parents worked. My grandparents were observant. They used two sets of dishes: one for meat and one for dairy. They also had two stoves. One of my mother's grandfathers was a rabbi. The grandmother hosted all the holidays. It was a large family of eleven siblings on one side, ten on the other. Except for the parent of a cousin, and my mother's parents, none of them came back from the death camps.

My grandparents stayed in Belgium. My mother was an only child, very close to her mother, less to her father. My grandmother died when I was four years old, my mother was then twenty-nine. She never recovered from the loss of her mother.

The relationship with my grandfather was more difficult. Both grandparents had been ill, but my grandfather suffered even more from his loss. My grandmother was the axis of the family. Her death foreshadowed the disintegration of family unity. I didn't know her well. I have some memories because I came to Belgium when I was two and a half. She was a cheerful person, very opulent, affectionate, the typical "Yiddishe Mame." My mother resembles her father.

When I was small, my mother never played with me. She never came down to my level, but tried bringing me up to hers. She never played any board games. When I was older, she agreed to play "Scrabble," but she disliked it so much that I stopped playing with her. It put her in a very bad mood, she would become agitated.

My mother spent a great deal of time teaching me to read and write. When I started school I could read and write, this made my mother very proud. My American grandmother was horrified. She said, "My God, you stuff that child's small head."

I never wondered why she didn't play. I had no way to compare her to American-born mothers, she was my model. We had very little social life, we always lived in an isolated fashion. My mother was twenty-one when she came to America but she never became integrated in the United States.

Moreover, my mother never participated in meetings of "hidden children." I saw a program on television entitled "The Hidden Children." In it a woman raised the topic of relationships with her children and her husband. It bowled me over. The next day, I phoned my mother. She said she knew of those meetings, a friend had told her about them. I didn't know that there was an organization in Paris called "Hidden Children." My mother was hidden with a Catholic family; she went to mass every Sunday, she wore a cross around her neck. She told us that when she came out of hiding, for her the word "Jewish" meant "death." My grandparents were very preoccupied, managing this child who wore a cross, who no longer wanted to speak Yiddish. They tried to resume celebrating the Jewish holidays, but they stopped because there was no one left, and they mourned the death. My grandmother consulted an organization seeking advice as to what to do with her child. My grandparents registered my mother in a Jewish school and a Jewish youth group. She went to Israel for several months when she was seventeen.

My mother's fear of abandonment related to her not knowing whether her parents were alive or not. Would they come back one day to get her? I visualized images that I invented. For instance, my mother on the threshold of the house in the village where she was hiding, holding an American flag while the liberating tanks rolled through. I imagined this little girl sitting at the door, waiting for her parents day after day. Thus, my mother must have told me things that conjured up these pictures.

In my opinion, what has been transmitted to me, and what I am trying to unload, is not the fear of abandonment; I don't think that such feelings are part of my big anxieties, of which I have quite a few. What I am trying to discard is this black vision of the world, a world where happiness is not accessible, where all the events that I confront are presented in a negative manner. Somewhere in my psyche I don't allow myself to be happy.

If any of my actions did not conform to my mother's wishes, she made me understand that she felt that it was because I wanted her to suffer, to hurt her; I was her tormentor. My father was very passive. I was also passive and submissive to my parents' authority.

My father comes from a secular family. I was brought up without any religion whatsoever. My mother rejects anything that has to do with religion. My father was not interested either, not concerning the faith, nor any of the traditions. I knew nothing about Jewish history, nor did I know the traditions, or the history of Israel. It was all blocked out. When I lived in the United States it was still OK, because the New York City environment was very Jewish. Thus I knew the significance of *Rosh Hashanah*[1] and *Yom Kippur*,[2] because my class at school was full of Jewish children who were absent on those days. I knew about *Pesach*[3] and *matzah*.[4]

I was sixteen when I came to France. Suddenly, I understood that I was part of a minority. In New York we told everyone that we were Jews, but not in Paris. That is when I went on a quest for an identity. I started to discover politics. In 1973, when I was sixteen, the Yom Kippur war was raging in Israel. I joined a movement where I worked on fund-raising. I began to build "individuality." I started to wear my mother's Star of David that she gave me because she no longer wanted it. This drove her into hysterics. It bothered her terribly that I would wear an exterior sign of Judaism. I couldn't reason with her, it was impossible. But at sixteen, one believes that one still can reason with people. I no longer have such discussions with her. I wear a *chai*--the Hebrew letters that stand for life. When I am with her, I hide my necklace because I don't want to get my mother angry, it doesn't do any good; I cannot convince her, nor can she convince me. She claims that wearing such a symbol is provocative.

My mother is full of contradictions. She wants us to be Jewish, but for her, being Jewish means the *Shoah*, the Holocaust. For me this isn't so, and it doesn't please her. I am not observant, but I love the Jewish traditions. I am interested in the history, therefore I inform myself. I participate in Jewish movements, and so does my husband. He made *alyiah* in Israel as part of a youth movement. He went into the army. He isn't observant, but for all the holidays we are with his family. My parents don't even know the date when Yom Kippur is celebrated. I don't work on that day, and even if it is the only holiday that I considered really a religious one; I fast. This may not make sense, but it is my way, and I find that what I do suits me. I take what I need from the traditions. I do *Pesach*,[3] *Rosh Hashanah*,[1] *Purim*,[5] *Succoth*,[6] and *Chanukah*.[7] I don't do *Shabbat*, because this I consider strictly religious. The language that has to do with faith--the prayers—doesn't move me. On the other hand, I am very interested and attached to the reasons for these events. I have my own interpretation as to what they commemorate. I memorialize my belonging to the Jewish people, its history, its language, and its traditions.

I am not enough of a Zionist to settle in Israel. I don't feel at home there. In terms of culture, I feel more French than Israeli, but I strive for Israel's security. I am extremely interested in all that is happening there.

I am always very careful not to use the word "Jew" when my mother is present. We have always been very protective of her; she demanded it, that's how it was to be. We considered her fragile, she no longer had her mother, and she was an emigrant far from her family, lacking attachments. My mother was very thin; this gave her the appearance of a child, evoking feelings of protection in us. She weeps a lot, like a child; she has outbursts of anger, also like a child. She is totally unable to deal with abstractions. Logic and mathematics are beyond her; she is much more at ease in a literary gathering, but never in a logical and objective system. She only functions on the emotional level, resorting to blame, forced relationships, emotional blackmail.

I never asked my mother to stop; I endured, I submitted, until age forty-three. I have just started to realize what vicious effects this has had on me because I was in a precarious situation in my personal life. I never understood that this could be the origin. I could never imagine or accept this. From the day I started to foresee that my mother's behavior could be the source of my difficulties, I took the phone book and looked for a woman psychiatrist. I wanted her to be a Jewish woman who practiced in my neighborhood. Otherwise, due to my crazy schedule, I wouldn't have the time to go to see her. That is how I found this woman and I have been her patient for the past six months. Also, I haven't seen my mother in all this time.

I think that if today I am in therapy, it is because of a lack of confidence in myself. When I was a child in school, I remember that my lack of confidence lasted until I was fourteen; I was shy, and so frightened. It seems to me that the reason I was such a good student was due to my fear of not succeeding. I was always first in my class, constantly afraid that my parents wouldn't be proud of me. I worried that my teachers would give me bad grades. When I had to recite my lesson, even though I knew it by heart,

I trembled from head to foot. I was always very intimidated by authority and by my parents.

So, at fourteen, I decided that this was such a handicap for me that I undertook for myself a kind of personal therapy. I looked to rid myself of this anxiety I suffered in regard to my teachers. I imagined them being two years old and wetting their pants. That was the way that, from one day to the next, I was cured of this shyness. It was gone overnight. It freed me in regard to my teachers, but not in relation to my parents.

At puberty, I rebelled and became a tomboy. My father is very tall, and I was tall for my age. I played basketball and volleyball, and I developed a masculine appearance. This was at the beginning of the 1970s, "unisex" was in fashion. I took advantage of this unisex mood in order to pass for a boy. This enabled me to be more comfortable with boys. I was ill at ease with boys, except in a sports environment. This disappeared with some maturity. Afterward, I had more friends who were boys than friends who were girls. Now I find it more interesting to be among women.

In my professional environment, everyone makes fun of me because I only have women on my team, whereas ten years ago, I had only men.

I have developed a presence that is far from reality. I give the illusion that I am sure of myself. I engage in public speaking, I give lectures. Yet no one knows what is happening inside of me, because deep down I totally lack confidence.

In contrast, my sense of independence is very developed. But while I was growing up my mother fostered a total dependency. I depended on her affection; when I didn't conform, she refused her love, or she stopped speaking to me. It was emotional black mail. I had to comply again otherwise I suffered.

My mother always wanted to appear younger than her age. She was terribly afraid of getting older. Her clothes are the latest of what is in style. She was always proud to be my "friend." She would lead me to confide in her, until I discovered that taking her into my confidence was turning against me. That is how our first break-up occurred. She made me believe that she was my friend. I felt I had been wronged and I stopped confiding in her.

When I reached adolescence I started distancing myself from her. We lived in the United States, but my mother rejected everything that was American. I had no right to speak English, or to have American friends. When I spoke English in her presence it was with a French accent so as not to shock her. I wasn't allowed to have American soft drinks, or American food; or to see American films and television programs.

My mother married an American, but she tried to change him into someone French. She succeeded in having him immigrate to France. He became French, heart and soul. My mother knows how to manipulate people; she vaporizes them, she changes them in her image.

Does she have identity problems?

I believe that her dream is to be French, an atheist, and to have no label.

When we lived in the States I discovered very late that my mother was Belgian. She always said that she was French. French was better than Belgian. I never wondered why my grandfather lived in Brussels. In France, she also never says that she is Belgian.

When I got married I discovered that my mother's first name was Esther. Everyone called her Astride, even when she was a child. She used her second name; *Astride* is not Jewish, like *Esther.*

The Swedish name, Astride, became very popular in Belgium because of the very beloved Queen Astride, the wife of Leopold III.

My grandmother would say to my mother, "You are my queen." However, my mother doesn't want to be Belgian, she doesn't want to be named Esther, and she doesn't want to be Jewish.

My mother's rapport with my American grandparents was bad. My father was forty-two years old when he changed countries. He had two children; my brother was twelve and I was sixteen. He had always lived in the United States and he had never worked anywhere else.

My parent's relationship was not good. In the States, my mother was ill; she suffered from having lost her mother. My grandfather came to live with them; it was hell and he returned to Belgium. My mother was chronically depressed, and my father couldn't stand it. They fought continuously. All my mother's relationships are violent. No one finds mercy in her eyes. Her criticism challenges one's understanding. Everything is painted black, she only sees people's faults. She destroys all her connections.

I have identity problems. In America I was French; in France I am American. I am always different. In certain ways I proclaim this difference, it makes me distinct and somewhat special. I must find a balance between what was transmitted to me, and what is necessary for me.

The day before yesterday, my eight-year-old son Leo and I were in Amsterdam. He requested that we visit the house of Anne Frank because he saw the film about the young girl. He belongs to a group of *Eclaireurs Israelites de France* (a movement similar to Jewish Boys Scouts), which meets every Sunday. I try to transmit to him Jewish values. I don't have much time, but I must be vigilant about my mother's influence on him. I worry that she will sway his desire to be Jewish. Therefore, it is imperative that I show him the joyful aspects of Judaism through holidays: the Chanukah candles, the songs, and the hut on the balcony for Succoth. Leo will be going to summer camp with his youth movement. I give him the positive aspects that will give him equilibrium. I think that if my mother didn't underline for him the negative perspective, I would give him more details about the *Shoah*. I don't emphasize the subject at home, he gets plenty of it when he visits my mother.

Do you think that you'll speak to him about the Shoah when your mother is gone?

I do speak to him now, but my approach is not complete. The information I transmit to him would be more detailed if my mother were absent.

I am not a mother hen, I let my son be. On that subject, my mother reproaches me constantly. She tells me that I am a bad mother, that I work too much outside the home; it is very insidious. She says, "The way you handle your son is intolerable." Whereas everybody compliments me on how I guide his education, my mother finds only fault. She is a mother hen to him by being overprotective.

My mother never learned how to swim, therefore she is afraid to be in water. We always had prohibitions; she feared for herself, for my father, for my brother, for me. She fears everything, she has the impression that danger lurks everywhere.

I had a first relationship that lasted six years. My parents did everything to separate me from this boy. My mother is very manipulative, and she easily influences my father. I think that I would have broken up with him earlier if my parents hadn't tried to interfere. But I was stubborn, and so I held on to show them that I was right.

They repeated this maneuver with my brother. He has been living with someone for the past ten years, my parents have never given up the idea of separating them. My brother, who is now thirty-nine years old, just became the father of a little girl, but he didn't marry her mother. He ruined his life on our parents' account. He cannot make a life for himself, and working with my father isn't helpful.

In terms of my husband, in the beginning my parents were very positive. However, little by little, my mother's critical nature started to make trouble. It became an enterprise of destruction; gradually she denigrated his image. My husband has a great respect for family. For him it is a sacred bond, so he kept quiet. However, he revolted against me, but I didn't understand that it was because I accepted the situation. It took me a long time to understand that our relationship was becoming more and more stressed and risky. I played a role that lowered me in his esteem. I was submissive, I accepted what my parents inflicted upon us, and I didn't react.

I had very heated discussions with my parents regarding my brother. He isn't married because his partner isn't Jewish. I told them that it was unjust to impose such a rule when we had no Jewish life at home, that we had had no Jewish education. My brother never had a Bar Mitzvah; we knew nothing about Jewish traditions, nor did we know anything about the holidays. My parents were terribly piqued that I could say such things. As far as they were concerned, we had had a Jewish education. For them, learning about the *Shoah* is a Jewish education, that is our identity. They declared, "How can you say this when you know from where we came since the time you were very small? You knew what happened to us, you knew that we lost so many of our loved ones."

For them, this is what it means to be Jewish. I cannot make them understand that this is not what develops a sense of being Jewish, that my brother received nothing. I was an adolescent at a time when people were militant, when politics were important. There were events where one took positions. My brother is four years younger than I. He belongs to another age group that is rather materialistic, a group that is in the habit of having instant gratification. He didn't experience the events that marked me.

As I said, my mother is full of contradictions. She wants us to marry Jews; she teaches my son Yiddish words. She doesn't like Israel because the people there don't speak Yiddish. As far as she is concerned, the "Pieds Noirs" (Jews of North African origin) aren't Jews because they didn't experience the *Shoah*; they are Arabs. My father-in-law died ten years ago. He wasn't Jewish. But my mother-in-law, who is Jewish, had a good marriage. My parents' relationship with her is cool. My mother finds her uneducated, she says she has an accent.

My mother managed an excellent "gloss" in terms of her education in order to cover her modest origins. She has the *baccalauréat;* she is also qualified as a dental hygienist; she reads a great deal. On the other hand, she only deals with what she finds interesting. In politics, in history, in technical subjects, she knows nothing. People who are interested in what she deems unworthy don't deserve her attention.

Are you proud to be Jewish?

I know who I am, and I say so. One can be proud of what one

has constructed. I am Jewish by accident. I can say that I am glad to be Jewish; I am happy because of the richness it brings me, of the difference, of the sense of belonging. But I cannot say that I am proud.

Do you worry that what happened to your mother could happen again?

I am very attentive and active. I don't believe that the *Shoah* could be repeated because of modern methods of communication. I believe that there exists a vigilance and a resistance that is well organized and in place.

I have often experienced anti-Semitism. I don't advertise that I am Jewish when I am not asked, but I don't hide it. As I said, I wear a *"Chai;"* many people recognize this Hebrew letter and understand the word that it represents. Some think it is my initial, or a little dog. Some individuals have made anti-Semitic comments in my presence, because they didn't know that I am Jewish. This has happened, largely in my professional life, and often by people whose prejudices surprised me. I would discover their bigotry as we gathered during a break for coffee at an executives' meeting. I saw them then in a different light, which kept me from pursuing a normal relationship with them.

At these times I have reacted in a very forceful manner. Tolerance is a value that I have prized as an individual, and this feeling is probably exacerbated because I am Jewish. I believe in these values, and I defend them. If someone makes racial observations-- and this happens, against Arabs or Africans--I react in the same manner. I have a very keen sensitivity in this matter.

This is a special time in my life because I am engaged in a difficult journey. I would say that I am at a point in my life where today I affirm my identity with serenity. My relationship with my coworkers is on an even keel. I have a circle of friends, therefore a rich social life. My married life is on the mend because I have made order of my personal dysfunction, I have an excellent relationship with my son.

The rest I must destroy and reconstruct--that is to say, I must reconstruct my relationship with my mother as well as with my father. This is a very painful process, I believe that it will be long.

For forty years I have been carrying profoundly anchored stigmas in my vision of the world, my environment, and myself.

The fact that I haven't seen my mother for the past six months makes me terribly unhappy. I became ill, and I didn't know that it was a breakdown. My mother found out, and chose that time to create a break-up with my husband. She claimed that for years she had suffered from his actions. On that day, my mother quarreled with my husband. She told him that she no longer wanted to see him. This aggravated my condition even more, and since then I haven't heard from her. I told her that it would be better not to see one another for the time being. She respects this wish, which I find very strange. I would have loved for her to protect me this once, the only time in my life when I really needed it. Instead she destroyed me, she gave the last blow.

I never discussed matters with my brother while growing up. I started speaking with him later because he had problems with my parents due to his rapport with his partner. That is when we started to untangle the knots in the relationship and the behavior of my mother and father. We agree, we have the same vision. This is something that only he and I can share.

My brother's baby girl is six months old. We don't see each other very often. I don't want him to come without his partner. My mother was angry that I would invite them together.

Your mother must be very unhappy.

Of course. She expresses her pain, but she also transmits it to others. She doesn't realize that she never stops, and I refuse to bear it any longer. I cannot reason with her. I had great difficulty in accepting that I couldn't speak with my mother. I knew that she wouldn't understand what I wanted to tell her. I finally understood that what was most important was for me to say it. I did it once two months ago. First of all, I told her that I loved her, but that I wanted a different relationship, one that is not forced and based on domination.

Do you think that your mother behaves as she does because she was formed by her experience as a child?

I believe it to be the cause. She is ill, but she has never agreed to be treated, and therefore she has never understood what bothers her. As far as she is concerned, others are in the wrong, she is always right. She lives in a world where this is her truth. She is also very violent in her speech.

She got angry easily while I was growing up. I was already big when she stopped hitting me. Her verbosity hurt me more than her blows; she is very cruel. Now I resist by distance; this is the first therapy. I must say that I am starting to miss her.

I stopped sending my son to my parents. I found it abnormal that my mother had no relationship with me, her daughter, yet she wanted to see my son. Besides, she forbade him to speak of his parents; he was not allowed to mention our names. I didn't want to submit him to such treatment. Then they sent me an email asking me if I would accept that my son see his grandparents. I said yes, but I still find the relationship abnormal.

I have said many harsh things about my mother. It is not her truth, it is mine. I have given the matter a lot of thought for a long time. It has become a subject of permanent reflection and introspection. However, should my mother make a gesture toward me, I would go to her. Not only does she have influence on me, I am in her grasp.

NOTES:

1. Rosh Hashanah. See page 58 note 6.
2. Yom Kippur. See page 143 note 2.
3. Pesach. See page 57 note 1.
4. Matzah. Unleavened bread eaten at Pesach.
5. Purim. Reading of the scroll of Esther. Commemorates victory over oppression of Jews in ancient Persia.
6. Succoth. Jewish harvest festival.
7. Chanukah. Jewish festival of lights.

GABRIELA

MANY TIMES I WISHED I WEREN'T JEWISH.
I KEPT THINKING,
"WHY DO I NEED TO JUSTIFY MYSELF?
WHY DO I HAVE THIS BURDEN,
THIS SUFFERING OF THIS PEOPLE?"

Sometimes opportunities for research present themselves in unexpected ways. Such was the case in my meeting Gabriela after I had returned to the United States from Israel and France in the summer of 2000.

On a hot Sunday morning in August, my husband and I drove to Concord, Massachusetts to swim at Walden Pond. Sitting on stone slabs in a remote area on the banks of the pond, we noticed two young people who had stopped on the path and were peeking at our spot. We invited them to share it with us. The young man accepted immediately and got ready for a dip, but the young woman worried that the water was too cold. She said that she was used to warm water, being Italian, and having lived nearly all of her life in Rome. Now she lived and studied in Israel and swam in the warm Mediterranean.

"Oh," I said, "how interesting. I just returned from Israel,." whereupon she inquired as to the purpose of my visit there. I outlined my project and asked her whether she too was the child of a hidden child. When she replied in the affirmative, I proposed that she participate in my study.

At first she declined, then agreed hesitatingly. We made plans to meet at my house.

The following week Gabriela came on the day of her thirty-first birthday. She explained that the American young man who was with her when we met was a friend she knew in Israel whose family had offered her their hospitality during her stay in Boston.

Gabriela was nervous, but controlled her emotions. We proceeded with the interview.

I don't remember how old I was when I first learned about the Holocaust, I think that the subject was always with me. My mother had a cousin to whom she was very close. He survived Auschwitz. This cousin's father died in Auschwitz.

I didn't want to hear or speak about the Holocaust. I remember that when my mother watched the film *Shoah*,[1] I was very concerned. I disliked watching violence; I abhorred cruelty even toward animals. As a child I became a vegetarian, and my parents, who were extremely protective of me, worried about my nutrition. They forbade my watching television if the program contained any brutality. However, they didn't object to my watching *Shoah*. I remember seeing corpses.

I know very little about my parents' experience in hiding during those terrible war years. Their story is blurred in my mind because of my ambivalent feelings: I wanted to know, and yet I didn't want to. I remain that way to this day. Yet lately I have been asking more questions. My mother never spoke about her past. My grandmother told me that my grandmother's friend, a Christian woman, hid her, together with my mother and my mother's sister. My grandfather didn't hide; he went around with false identity papers. I think that he stayed at the apartment. I don't know how long they were hidden, I plan to ask them.

I know that my father's mother hid him in a convent; he was very young. She had four children whom she hid in different places. The nuns were mean to my father; they didn't give him enough to eat. My grandmother brought him food, and the nuns would take it from him. One of the stipulations for being hidden in that convent was to supply two ration cards. I don't know if and how much my grandmother had to pay as well. I have the impression that she paid. When my father got sick, they wouldn't keep him; they sent him back at the risk of his life.

My father never spoke about his stay at the convent, I only know it from my grandmother. She said that my father had artistic talents in visual art, that he was made to draw and paint crucifixes. I feel upset when I think that he had to do that. My grandmother told me that she was so concerned with food, she became a compulsive food buyer when the war ended. My father follows the same pattern, he overeats. I think that this is connected to his childhood.

My grandmother, on my father's side, also told me that a rumor circulated in the Jewish community that Jewish children were hidden in the Vatican for a lot of money. Also, they risked being converted.

Did the nuns try to convert your father?

I don't think so. However, my grandmother was very upset with them, she wasn't grateful. But on my mother's side, my grandmother was very grateful to her friend who hid her with her two children. This friend risked her life to save them. They stayed hidden during the round-up of the Jews of Rome.

Where was your grandfather then, the one who walked the streets with false papers?

Again, I don't know, but now I will inquire. When I was growing up, I hardly ever questioned my parents. I think that I was afraid of the answers. I just wanted to remove this story from my life-- it was too painful for me.

Yet, did you feel that you could have asked had you wanted to, that there weren't any secrets in your household?

I sensed that my father would be uncomfortable if questioned.

Did it occur to you that he would have liked you to question him, to show interest?

I don't think so; he didn't want to talk, and he probably knew that I didn't want to hear. He was protecting me, and I was protecting him as well as myself. My father keeps silent about certain issues. He refuses to discuss anything unpleasant.

My mother referred to the past sporadically, maybe at family gatherings. Sometimes I heard the family speak of how awful it was when they were forbidden to go to school. One aunt recalled that her best girlfriend would no longer speak to her. My grandmother sometimes said something when it was connected to a present-day occurrence, such as my father's eating habits. Or she would refer to his time in the convent, saying that they made him do "all this work there." My mother said explicitly that she wanted to forget about that time. When someone asked her to recall, she refused. She didn't want to remember and neither did my father.

Then my mother got very involved in an organization called "Former Deportees Association." Her cousin, the one who survived Auschwitz, became its president. She wanted to help him. It wasn't a very powerful establishment.

The Italian government didn't do much for death camps survivors. Politicians invited survivors to speak: they used them for their own political gains. I was disgusted with their maneuvering.

I went to Warsaw in 1994 for the anniversary of the Warsaw Ghetto uprising. I was a member of the presidium of the European Union of Jewish Students. People came from all over Europe. At the ceremony I learned for the first time all about the *Shoah*. For the first time I read Primo Levi; I think that his writing is the most powerful. I often put myself in all of the Jews' places, even more than just my parents'. For the past few years I have had nightmares about the camps. I have had dreams of being persecuted, that neo-Nazis were looking for me in the streets of Rome.

The power of the media is so strong. I thought that the Benigni film *Life is Beautiful* was in bad taste. I was present when Benigni spoke in Jerusalem. I stood up and said that this was a revisionist film, it was about changing the memory of the experience. This is subtle revisionism, it is manipulative, and it is a fairy tale with a specific theme.

How has your parents' silence affected your life? When we met, it seemed to me that just the thought of what they must have gone through brought tears to your eyes. Did you identify with them, or was it the notion of what happened to the Jewish people as a whole that pained you so?

Of course I relate to my parents' experience. However, the whole of the Jewish people's suffering was my concern. I am totally concerned with the Holocaust, it has affected my life, entirely, and it is a constant presence.

Recently, I have understood that it is impossible to become involved with all the suffering. I try to educate others through my own pain and history. I cried thinking about my parents because the ache is very deep; I never really dealt with it. Certain matters bother me so. For instance, my mother never throws any food away. I say to her, "Mom, you don't need to keep food that you don't like, we aren't in the war anymore." She replies, "I hope that you never have to have such an experience." My father throws things away. He has the opposite reaction. She needs to save, but I think that he appreciates the luxury of being able to discard what seems superfluous. My mother's ways bothered me a lot when I was a child. She would eat everything, and I objected to her spirit of sacrifice.

As a child, I remember seeing my mother crying, but she wouldn't tell me why. She often got depressed, but I think that she never admitted it. I inherited this tendency from her. Again, we never talked about it.

I grew up hearing my father shouting in his sleep. He often had nightmares. My mother got used to it. For me it was clearly an indication of danger, but I never dared ask him about what he dreamed. My anxieties regarding danger are related to hearing my father shout, but I never spoke about it with anyone. My inner life, or my parents', was never a topic of discussion with them.

I have an emotional family where everyone cries easily, including the men, who aren't supposed to cry. My father and my brother have a tendency to get emotional. That is why I felt it was too painful to speak; it was too difficult to open up, too threatening.

My parents gave me so much. I desperately want them to be happy after having had such difficult childhoods.

My father fears abandonment, he can't be alone. My mother is always with him, and to this day he never wants us to be alone in the house. My parents would come home for meals from the other side of the city to be with us. This need to be present is also why, in my relationships with men, I request their presence and don't want to be left out of any part of their lives. Although my parents were nearly always present, I think that I grew up with this fear of abandonment. When I was a young child and my parents were working, my brother and I were never alone, my aunt looked after us.

I was always in public school among Christian children. Some of them asked me whether it was true that my God was not a merciful one? In Italian slang *rabbi* means a stingy person. When children insulted each other, they would use the word *Jew* or *rabbi*. When I was seven or eight years old the family was at the beach. One of the children with whom I was playing remarked that certain people acted in certain ways "because they were Jews." I remember the incident very clearly because it hurt me so. I didn't say anything. I used to cry. Now I wouldn't keep quiet, I would respond on the spot.

I hid my identity in school from ages six to ten. I had the same teacher for five years. One day she called on me, and it shocked me terribly when she said, "Gabriela, tell us why during the entire week you don't eat bread." My distress must have been obvious, because she changed the subject immediately. I felt so ashamed because I was different. There were no other Jewish children in the class. One day I confided in my best friend, I told her that I was Jewish. She replied, "Why don't you speak Jewish, were you born in Israel?" At age six I had to explain what Judaism was, and that I was Italian, exactly like her.

I had a hard time in school when I was seventeen. There were some people there who were right wing. My best friend befriended some of them, and from one day to the next she didn't speak to me again.

Many times I wished I weren't Jewish; I kept thinking," Why do I need to justify myself? Why do I have this burden, the suffering of this people?" To my mind, religion created conflict, I was against it. I asked. "Why am I different?" I didn't want to be Jewish, but I never denied it. When I discovered the beauty of Judaism I found my Jewish Identity in a positive way.

At home we celebrated the High Holidays and all the major Jewish holidays. For Shabbat we had *Kiddush* [2] but no candles. At *Chanukah* we lit candles, but we also had a Christmas tree. My grandmother on my father's side didn't like that. My brother and I had a private teacher who instructed us for our *Bar* and *Bat Mitzvahs*[3]. I learned no Jewish history until I was old enough to investigate for myself. At seventeen, I joined an Italian Jewish youth movement.

In my first year in college I participated in a demonstration for students rights. We went by the Synagogue in Rome and some students threw eggs against the façade, and I was there. I was part of this movement! There were thousands of people marching, but no one tried to stop these desecrators. Many anti-Semitic incidents took place. I went to Israel when I finally couldn't take it any longer.

At Hebrew University in Jerusalem I took a class about the Holocaust. There were many Germans there and we had some discussions. When I was making a point, one German young woman was offended, she felt so guilty. She thought that it was so nice of her to come to Israel. I wasn't willing to buy this, to clear her conscience by coming to Israel. I told her that she didn't do me any favors, she should just accept what I had to say.

I feel bad about the whole European Christian culture and their persecution of Jews throughout the ages. I think of my ancestors in the ghettos, the expulsion in Spain, the pogroms in Poland and Russia.

My family overprotected me, I had problems stepping into adult life. Recently I told this to my parents, although in a nice way, because I wanted to thank them for the love they gave me. I said that I found it hard to be independent in Israel, I always thought of home. I am very demanding in relationships. I have trouble choosing a partner.

My life has been quite a journey. If I were to define myself right now, I would say that I am Jewish. There is nothing in my life that I am more certain of.

<hr />

Gabriela sent me email messages and phoned me several times from Israel. She is married and has two little girls.

NOTES:

1. The film entitled *Shoah*. Nine hour film about the Holocaust by Claude Lanzman, completed in 1985.
2. *Kiddush*. See page 131 note 4.
3. *Bat Mitzvah*. Coming of age ceremony for Jewish girls at age 12 or 13.

BRACHA

*I WAS ASTOUNDED AT THE RESOLUTENESS IT TOOK
IN ORDER TO SURVIVE. I WAS SURPRISED TO LEARN THAT
SUCH A YOUNG CHILD WOULD REMEMBER SO MUCH.*

Acquaintances who read my memoir, Unveiled Shadows, *passed the
book on to a friend whose background is similar to mine. He too had been
a hidden child; he was also born in Vienna and fled from that city with his
family to Belgium in 1938, the year of the Anschluss.[1]*

*I invited two of this man's daughters to testify as to their experience
growing up as a child of a hidden child. The following is one daughter's
contribution.*

*We met one early spring evening at my house. Bracha was then twenty-
four years old; she worked in advertising and lived in Boston.*

I asked her what she knew about her father's past.

I have heard through him what happened to his parents and
relatives. Every time I hear the story, different details emerge.
Sometimes visitors may question him about his youth, and that
will start an anecdote. It often happens when we have company
for Friday night Shabbat dinner and we are getting to know each
other. Sometimes the people are foreign born, sometimes they
are Americans, and they are often new in town. Sometimes a
new detail of my father's experience will emerge due to a remark

during the conversation. If I am not clear about a certain episode, I question him after the company has left.

In school when we had Holocaust Studies and I had to write an essay, I would ask my father about his experience. I also asked my grandfather, who is my mother's father, and who would give me a historical explanation, rather than a personal one.

My paternal grandparents came from Poland. My grandfather went to Vienna to study. I am not sure about my grandmother. My grandparents were observant. My father was their only child. My father is very willing to talk about his life, he even made a tape for one of the broadcasting companies, but it was never aired. This was before the Spielberg Foundation[2] made tapes of the stories of survivors.

My father used to correspond with the people who hid him. Recently, I asked him the name of the town. I met girls who are from France and I was curious whether they came from the same place--right now I can't remember the name. I know that the family started out in Vienna, then they went to Belgium, but my father was hidden in France. The family didn't live in France, they were fleeing Belgium from the advancing German troops and were caught. I don't know what year.[3]

My grandmother and her mother were together throughout the war. They were taken to a slave labor camp. Somehow, through the partisans in the underground, my grandmother knew of my father's whereabouts. My grandfather was taken away, but I don't know exactly where or when.

Do you ever discuss this with your siblings?

It doesn't usually come up. My oldest sibling is thirty-one. There are seven of us: six girls and one boy, the youngest is eleven. My mother was forty-nine when my youngest sister was born. There is an eight-year gap between the second youngest and the youngest. The rest of us are fairly close, about a year and a half to two or three years apart.

My father made a family tree with all the names. He doesn't get emotional when he speaks of his childhood. Some aspects are very sad, others aren't. Therefore he must experience a mix of feelings.

My mother is American born. She was very young during the war. She has some recollections of the community discussing the subject and talking about taking care of refugees.

Does your mother ever discuss your father's reactions? Does she ever mention that he has nightmares?

No, I don't think so. One time she said that he had nightmares. I am not sure whether it was when he was a child, or after they were married--if it was during the war, or after. I don't know.

I grew up in Boston. I went to Maimonides Day School[4] through the twelfth grade, and then I went to Israel for one year to study at the Seminary in Jerusalem. Afterward, I studied in the business school of Stern College in New York City.

In school we always observed *Yom HaShoah*.[5] However, the real program of the formal teaching of the subject, the Holocaust, began in fifth grade.

At the start, the students were shown movies of the camps--the barracks, people suffering, and corpses. The films showed how terrible the people looked when they were liberated. We saw pictures of city streets where explosions went off. The end always showed Israel, clips from the war of independence; people being smuggled in by sea.

When I was in first grade, one of my sisters refused to go to school on *Yom HaShoah*. When she was exposed to the program for the first time, she couldn't deal with it, it upset her so. My parents wouldn't make her go because she was so disconcerted. When she got older she realized that this wasn't a good way to introduce the subject, especially at such a young age.

When you came home from school after viewing these films, did you speak to your father about what you saw?

Probably, I don't remember exactly.

Did your parents comfort you?

I don't remember any discussions. We saw a lot more in junior high. My parents felt that we ought to know that this is, what happened, it was important. However, they didn't think that it was the best way to teach the subject.

Did you ask your father where he was at the time a certain camp was in existence? Did he interject himself into the story that you were shown?

I don't remember. However, at that time I didn't associate my father with what was shown. When I got older, I realized that this was part of his history.

In terms of my grandmother, I don't know if she was aware of all the details. I know that a few years ago, when I was in Israel, the Red Cross came to call. My father may have asked them to search for someone.

As I was growing up and people would come to the house, my father would speak of his experiences. The same man would come every Friday night for six or seven years. We would sit at the table until midnight, or one in the morning. I was probably in the sixth grade when I heard the story in depth for the first time. This man would ask questions, the rest of us would listen to my father's answers. We sometimes interjected questions of our own.

Were you upset by what you heard?

I was more amazed than upset--amazed about his courage. I recall this person asking many details: "What did you ask of the Lord? How did your mother keep in touch with you?" I was astounded at the resoluteness that it took in order to survive. I was surprised that such a young child would remember so much. He was so young at the time, but he was strong enough. One would think that a child would crumble without his parents, always knowing the presence of danger, always running.

The people who hid my father treated him exceptionally well. He was part of the family. There were two brothers and two or three sisters. They all belonged to the underground.

When the family was fleeing from the advancing German troops, they got to the unoccupied part of France. They were caught by the French Vichy militia and sent to a holding place. My father was left in the street, it was close to nightfall. One of the sisters saw him. I think that she first took him to another family.

He was transferred from one family to another. Then he wound up with the same family the whole time. Whenever there was a raid they would hide him in the mountains where they had relatives. He went to school the whole time. They never tried to convert him.

There were no secrets in my family, everything was very open, which is good. If survivors won't talk, how would anyone know what happened.

Do you think that your family being observant had something to do with this openness?

I think it had to do with my father's personality. Some people like to share.

Some people can't talk about their past because it is too upsetting. Also, they worry not only about unsettling their children; they are reluctant about reliving the times that were so difficult for them. You are one of the very few, among the children of child survivors whom I have interviewed, who can say that their parent's past was always openly discussed.

I wonder, if I had been able to speak to my grandmother, whether or not she would have discussed matters in such an open manner. My father realizes how privileged he was, in spite of losing a father and being separated from his mother. I don't think that he saw horrors. However, the matter of having to constantly be on the go must have had an effect on him. The fact that the family who hid him treated him so well was surely a great consolation.

Most likely, but imagine having your parents taken away and being left roaming the streets. How has your father's past affected your life?

I have always felt that we are here for a reason. So much had to happen in order for my father to be saved in such a peculiar way, and that is the reason that I am here. This makes me feel special. So many lives were destroyed; not everyone who survived could go on.

When you say that you feel special, what do you mean?

I feel special because my father is special; it comes through to me from him.

Do you attribute the fact that he was saved to other reasons than to cir-cumstance, do you believe that this was "meant to be"?

Yes, it is a miracle. My father was chosen to live, and as a result I am here today.

Do you attribute this to the Almighty having chosen him to survive?

Oh, definitely.

You don't think that it was mere luck, mere chance?

No, definitely not. However, I don't think anything is mere chance. I think that God is guiding everything, so whatever hap-pens, there is a reason that we often don't understand. Sometimes we can't expect to know, and sometimes we think we do.

What about the million and a half children that were murdered, many of them gassed upon arrival at the death camps? Do you think that God had anything to do which that?

Not necessarily. I mean,we have free will. However, there is a rea-son why it happened, but we can't understand it. I don't think that any human is capable of comprehending God's plans. However, even with all that happened, people survived by miracles. There has to have been a reason. I don't think that we'll ever understand such tragedy. Why did it have to happen to begin with? There has to be a reason, we just don't know it.

Your testimony is very different from anything that I have heard so far, and I have interviewed about a hundred witnesses. Of course, your faith is certainly wonderful. Have you read the work of Elie Wiesel? He writes that he lost his faith, but later found it again.

I read his work.

I am not denying your feelings, but to think that there was a reason for pious and wonderful people to perish and that it was in God's plan? I personally cannot accept that. The Holocaust cannot be figured out. It is so horrible that it cannot be explained.

But then today we find that horrible people come to power, how can one make sense of that! Power can convince other people to follow, just to destroy. People say that there was no God at the time of the Holocaust. Well, is there a God now? People are still killing people. God has the power, but humans decide what to do.

Then there are the innocents who cannot defend themselves. They should be protected. Personally, I think that God stays out of humans' actions. Free will or no free will, when you are in the hands of people who oppress you, your free will won't save you.

I agree.

Please tell me, did your father play with you when you were growing up?

Oh sure, he played with all of us. He pulled us in the carriage, he played ball, he rolled on the floor with us, he played monster, ghost, etc. I grew up in a harmonious household.

Again, what you say about your father playing with you is very different from most hidden children, who didn't play as they were growing up. Therefore, they seldom played with their own children. Your father probably played with the children of the people who hid him.

Yes, I think so. He was treated like a younger brother. He fit into the family in such a way.

Did he ever speak about his thoughts during that time? Did he wonder about the whereabouts of his parents and grandparents?

I don't know how much time he spent thinking. He went to school. He got shoes from his mother through the underground. We don't know how his mother, who was in a work camp, managed to do it.

My grandmother and her mother both survived, but neither of them is still living. I was five when my grandmother died, this was eighteen years ago. My father is now sixty-five.

Did you always want to be Jewish even when you heard what happened during World War II? Did you ever wish that you weren't, for fear that something similar might happen to you?

No, never. It never occurred to me. We cannot let history repeat itself, so we must be vigilant so that it won't. Throughout the ages the Jewish people have been persecuted. Unfortunately, we have plenty of sorrow in our history, but we have survived. I always wanted to be Jewish.

Did you experience anti-Semitism?

No, I don't think so. But then, I grew up very sheltered. I dress according to pious requirements, but I don't believe that I stand out. My brother wears a kipa,[6] though sometimes he covers it up with a baseball cap.

I was always in Jewish schools and in a Jewish environment. Therefore, I never encountered anything unpleasant. The environment of my place of work is Jewish as well. However, I worked at the Museum of Fine Arts, and there I was the only Jewish person in my department.

You are the only person among the people who contributed to this project who is strictly observant. This makes your testimony very different. You are very sure of yourself and don't share the feelings of insecurity that plague many of my other witnesses.

Did you ever feel that your father needed protection, since he had such a difficult childhood?

No. My father works for the State of Massachusetts, thus not a Jewish environment. He doesn't wear a *kipa* at work. When he eats he puts on a cap, when he prays he goes to a side room. Everyone knows that he is Jewish. Everyone wishes him happy holidays on Jewish festivals. When he comes home he puts on a *kipa*. I think that his not wearing one at work is generational. People of his generation always tried to blend in. It is different with the younger generation, probably for the last ten years. When I first realized that he doesn't wear a *kipa* in the office, I said to him, "Don't you think that everyone knows that you are Jewish, with a name like yours?" He said that he didn't want to be the only one wearing a kipa. Again, it may be generational, or having to do with his past. My brother always wears one, and is never self-conscious about praying before he eats. When someone wonders if he is talking to his food, he simply explains.

Do you feel anchored in American life? Would you always want to live in the United States?

First of all I feel that I am Jewish, and then American. I would love to live in Israel, but not right now, unless my whole family could come with me. We are very close and it would be hard for me to be away from them.

I would like to have a family, but would want to continue in my career when married. It seems to me that if one has the ability to support oneself, one should do so.

Who are your friends? Are they children of survivors? Are they children of hidden children?

Mainly not. Some are older; some are younger, mostly third-generation Americans.

Do you get along better with children of survivors whose background is similar to yours?

Not really. One of my friends' ancestors lived in Canada for several generations. They had to find a sixth cousin in order to locate a family member who was in Europe during World War II. She and I look at the Holocaust in a different manner. She went on "The March of the Living"[7] as a teenager. This is something that I would never do, I have no interest in seeing the death camps. It could be that she went because it strengthened her feelings. I suppose that this was her way of connecting.

When you knew that your friend was going on the "March of the Living," did you speak to her about the fact that you wouldn't want to go?

She was in the tenth grade, maybe the eleventh. I remember asking her why she would go on such a trip. She belonged to a youth organization where she was very active, and she received nearly a full scholarship to go. She considered it a learning experience. When she returned, it was obvious how affected she was by it. She had tons of pictures and all she wanted was to show them. It seemed to be her way of dealing with the horror. I feel that I don't need to experience this dread. I don't need to look for it in nightmares. My friend wanted to show her experience, but also, every time she showed the pictures to someone else, she relived some of her own emotions that built up within her. She was angry, yet emotional and upset.

Do you read books on the topic? What about films? Have you seen" Schindler's List," or "Europa, Europa?"

I read survivors' stories. Out of principle, I don't see any movies, ever. That is part of being observant. When I was younger, up to about the seventh grade, we had a television set. My younger brother was always watching and my parents didn't like it. So they got rid of the TV. But now there are computers--but that's a different story.

I read about "Schindler's List," I couldn't avoid it. I can discuss these movies as though I have seen them since everyone talks about them. I don't go to the theater, either. Occasionally, I go to concerts, Jewish ones. I have gone to the symphony.

Due to the fact that your family has no secrets, you were able to say it all. Also, even though your father was very young, he says that he remembers. In addition, he tries to search his mind to find what else he can tell you. Many people say that their parent doesn't remember, and would shrug off questions because he or she didn't want to talk about the past. This is where "secrets" come in. The fact that your father was so open about what happened, as well as your deep religious convictions, anchored you firmly in your personality. It seems to me that you have no feelings of insecurity. You are sure of who you are and what you want. You have no anxieties about the future, or of being socially ostracized.

Yes, I think that's right. Things can change, but right now, thank God, I have no such feelings.

Do you discuss those feelings or possibilities with your siblings? Do you speak of social situations, or the state of the Jewish people in general?

Sometimes these topics come up in conversations, yes. However, we don't usually philosophize. For instance, I don't vote, but I registered. My parents vote for president, maybe also for senator and representative. I am not sure.

The community definitely gives us a strong feeling of belonging. When I think of the crusades, I feel so terribly sad. Yet I always remember that no matter how hard it has been, survival perpetually followed. My pride in being Jewish is that we have been and will continue to be. How we endure depends on how we behave. We are lucky to live in America at this time where we are free to act according to our creed.

NOTES:

1. Anschluss The annexation of Austria to the German Third Reich in 1938.
2. Spielberg Foundation. See page 85 note 4
3. Exodus. See page 34 note 1.
4. Maimonides. Private Jewish day school in Brookline, Massachusetts, named after famous 12th Century Jewish philosopher.
5. Yom Hashoah. See page 109 lines 5-6.
6. Kipa. See page 121 note 7.
7. March of the Living. A two week trip for Jewish teenagers to Poland and Israel in memory of the Holocaust.

DISCUSSION

Wie man im Wald hinein ruft, so schallt es zurück. (The way one calls into the forest is how it echoes back.) My mother often recited this German proverb that, in effect, advises against the spreading of tales. This saying frequently emerged from my memory throughout the discussions with my interviewees because I found it applicable to these testimonies. The experience of the parents, echoed back in their children, whether transmitted verbally and intentionally, or silently and unintentionally.

The hidden children endured intense trauma in their young lives. Their offspring, in turn, suffered painful trepidation because their parents passed their anguish on to them. Often the children didn't dare ask, afraid of evoking painful memories for their parents. The parents didn't speak because they didn't want to remember, or because they had no memories. Often, they remained silent on purpose, thinking their secrecy would protect their children.

I found less distress among the children whose parents left the country where they had been hidden. One of the reasons for this difference is, I believe, that the people who remained in the same country had to periodically confront places throughout their cities that evoked anguishing memories. They often encountered sites where their loved ones were rounded up, then incarcerated, and ultimately transported to death camps. The feelings these places provoked in them were imparted to their offspring, whether unconsciously or consciously.

For example, one of my Belgian witnesses deplored her mother's driving past the concentration camp Breendonk, when they traveled together from Brussels to Antwerp.

"Why," she said, "do I always have to be reminded of the horrors that happened during the war?" Another revealed his uneasiness concerning his mother's allusions to the Gestapo headquarters on the Avenue Louise in Brussels each time this fashionable avenue was mentioned in conversation.

Sometimes there were similarities in the responses of the witnesses of the second generation. Other times they revealed differences in individual characters, dispositions, and circumstances. Some people deplored their parents' silence about their past. Others were overwhelmed by their elders' persistence in bringing up the topic; they wanted them to refrain at last from mentioning the subject. For some parents, that is to say the child survivors, the process of finally being willing to reconnect with their past took too long for their offspring. By the time the parents were ready to speak, their children wanted to move on, they needed to concern themselves with their own lives. A number of witnesses empathized profoundly with their parents; others felt bitterness and anger toward them. Yet, all of these children of hidden children were deeply affected by their elders' experience during the Holocaust.

One common reaction does stand out among the witnesses. They wanted to learn about their grandparents, they needed to fill this void in their lives. The witnesses yearned to learn of their families' fate. Some former hidden children knew nothing about themselves or their parents. The mother of one witness was an infant when her parents hid her with a gentile woman in Poland. Her long search brought no results, therefore she wanted to abandon her quest. However, her children urged her to keep searching by all means possible. They needed to know their grandparents' identity and what had become of them. Frequently parents refused to search. Then one of their children assumed the task, persevering until the result proved satisfactory.

The awareness of the Holocaust at a young age varied among the second generation witnesses I interviewed. In Israel, children heard about it throughout their lives, but did not always make the connection to their own family until they were older. In America, most witnesses learned about this calamity in synagogue religious schools, or in private Jewish schools. When families had few associations with Jewish communities, the children learned about the Holocaust only in their middle teens, or even later. Others acquired some anecdotes from their parents. Certain witnesses could not recollect at what age they found out, but they felt that they had always known. Some acquired the information in Jewish youth groups. One man learned of his mother's hidden childhood when she took him at a young age with his siblings to the convent to visit the nuns who had sheltered her. Sometimes a parent tried to tell, but often children were too involved with themselves to listen.

Many parents refused to speak because they wished to protect their children from learning of the evils of the world. They also were looking to shelter themselves from recalling the horror of the past. Other parents simply could not remember, or they resisted recollecting.

I found all the above-mentioned feelings prevalent among my fellow hidden children. These topics are raised frequently in workshops organized in the now yearly international gathering of child survivors of the Holocaust.

At times, when certain parents who had refused to speak finally broke the silence, they then raised the subject frequently and transmitted their pain intensely to their children. This continuous description ultimately burdened the children, and they would have liked not to hear about it any longer.

Some children refrained from inquiring, realizing that parents were fragile in regard to the subject and must be protected. They sensed the taboo of their parent's secret world. Yet then the silence mutated into emotions, and the children carried the anguish throughout a great part of their lives. One witness described how, upon entering a room, her mother and grand-mother abruptly stopped talking. Her exclusion engendered in her a grudge and suspicion. Somehow she perceived that they were discussing personal matters concerning the Holocaust. She wondered why they had secrets, why she was left out. In her imagination she considered all the possibilities. But in actuality, her imaginings surpassed the actual suffering of her elders' experience. In cases like this, not knowing was often more harmful than being enlightened.

Many of the hidden children did not play with their offspring. They rarely came down to their young children's level, but tried instead to bring them up to their own. This was because they had not played themselves when they were hidden. They missed this period in their development; they did not know how to relate to their children in play. I personally realized this phenomenon during a gathering of hidden children, in a workshop that was offered, entitled "Do you know how to play?" Since at the time I found the subject uninteresting, I did not attend. However, when I saw the results of the workshop, such as the drawings by the participants, I realized the purpose of the exercise. These adults had never experienced this elementary practice in their childhood. They had not drawn, and they had not played. I then understood why I had not played with my own children, for I too had missed that period of development.

Many of the witnesses had experienced this lack of participation by their hidden child parent in their own childhood. The above explanation helped to clarify the confusion they endured. The mother of a two year old expressed surprise and disappointment because her mother did not play with her grandchild. She was gratified by the clarification of her parent's experience. It relieved her resentment toward her mother.

Negative relationships with parents engendered deep guilt feelings in many witnesses. They struggled with difficulties in finding themselves, for they inherited their parent's vision of the world. They searched for a balance between what was transmitted to them and what was necessary for them to find peace. Some people strove to be good children; they tried not to give their parents difficulties. Others felt guilt for having had a happy childhood and adolescence when their parents had had such terrible experiences during theirs. Many sought out reasons for their existential pain. Why were they suffering? Why were they burdened with their parents' past?

Some witnesses could not free themselves of their parent's dark vision. They battled with this dilemma throughout their lives. In addition, it affected their relationship with their partners and spouses. Some young women had issues with their fathers who had been hidden children. These women had difficulties relating to the opposite sex, they lacked confidence in themselves and could not trust.

One interviewee, a daughter whose mother was open and spoke readily, was also burdened by the experience. In her quest for self, she identified with her mother and put herself in her mother's place. In addition, she worried about her mother's guilt feelings for having transmitted her own pain to her children. Yet this young woman felt only tenderness, compassion, and admiration for her mother.

A few witnesses derided the notion of their parents' hope that the generation of the witnesses would perpetuate the legacy of the Holocaust. Their elders encouraged them to carry on what the second generation referred to as "the torch." When I expressed bewilderment that such a wish should be scorned, one young woman reassured me that this remark should not be taken seriously. It was simply an expression of rebellion. For, they all carried "the torch," she said, whether willingly or not.

In their quest for identity many members of this second generation noticed that their degree of sensitivity exceeded the sense of awareness of their contemporaries, whose parents had no personal involvement with the Holocaust. They believed that their capacity for understanding and compassion was deeper.

The view of an orthodox young woman surprised me. She felt that divine providence had chosen her father to live. Therefore, in her opinion, her father was special and, being her father's offspring, she was special too. I questioned her regarding the lack of interference by "providence" in the murder of the one and a half million innocent children, as well as many very pious Jews. She answered that there are always reasons that we humans cannot understand. She was certain of her convictions and also of her sense of identity. Of all the witnesses in my study, she was the most positive. Her father's undoubting attitude was passed on to his daughter. Her description of the Orthodox community, and the closeness and support it provided, completed her sense of belonging. In contrast, many other witnesses toiled with identity problems. They always felt different from the people of the communities in which they lived, although sometimes they welcomed this separateness for they felt that it made them distinct. Some thought that life is easier for people whose parents are not survivors.

Parents who were hidden children share a phenomenon from their past. They experienced loved ones leaving and not returning. Therefore, they are wary about giving their own children their independence. Some witnesses thought that they had been overprotected while growing up, resulting often in a lack of confidence in themselves. Others rebelled against this, they believed that their parents were controlling and strict, and they chose not to acquiesce to their parents' wishes. On the other hand, some members of the second generation were left to look out for themselves and felt a lack of concern from their elders.

In terms of being anchored in their home countries, witnesses were of different opinions. Israelis were happy to remain in their country. Some interviewees perceived themselves to be citizens of the world, or simply European. Americans were satisfied being in the United States, although a few contemplated perhaps living in Israel some day. All supported the existence of the State of Israel, even though they may have chosen not to live there.

Witnesses discussed different occurrences regarding anti-Semitism. Two young women living in Israel who considered themselves Italian presented opposite personal experiences. Gabriela, who grew up in Rome, found intense anti-Semitism starting in grade school, so much so that she hid her identity. She experienced the same prejudice in secondary school, as well as in youth movements. On the other hand, Ofri, whose father considered himself Italian, and who grew up in Israel, had no such encounters even when she traveled in several countries in Western and Northern Europe. She stated that her Israeli passport engendered only positive attitudes. Yet her Israeli compatriot Tsilah experienced unpleasant reactions when she traveled in Austria. Other Israelis met with veiled and sometimes outright anti-Semitism when they went abroad. In the United States, Belgium, and France prejudices were mostly voiced in tactless jokes. Some witnesses never met with anti-Semitism because they attended Jewish schools throughout their education and circulated only in Jewish communities.

Most witnesses wanted to build productive lives, marry, and have a family. Others were terrified by the idea of offspring. These people felt they could not build anything, and that if they had children they would pass on their anguish to them.

Members of this second generation experienced being Jewish in diverse ways.

Those who were agnostic or atheist identified themselves as Jews because of the Holocaust. Some felt totally alienated from Jewish tradition, mainly because they never experienced it while growing up. They knew nothing about the richness of the tradition and history, and were absolutely not interested in learning about it. Others said that they did not believe in God. However, they appreciated the richness of their cultural heritage, they wanted to transmit this warmth to their children. One young woman felt that being an observant Jew was part of her identity, that without it she would be nothing. She wore a Star of David on a chain. This symbol gave her strength and marked the pain in her soul.

EPILOGUE

These testimonies bear witness to the consequences of experiences transmitted from one generation to the next. Yet, in many cases, when parents and their offspring communicated about these issues, they found peace between them. Oftentimes my interchanges with the second generation engendered for them new awareness, new comprehension, and new ideas regarding relationships with parents. One son, after speaking to his mother about our interview, invited me to meet her. They had debated and solved some of their problems and uncertainties. Both mother and son benefited from the discussion.

Some of the children of hidden children already had good communication with their parents before they testified. Still, they found that discussing the situation was beneficial, that in the interview they gained additional awareness of aspects of their relationships that they had not considered until then. They planned to speak to their parents regarding various details. Many, however, regardless of their improved relationship with their parents, remained perturbed by their difficult childhood.

Personally, my children and I gained immensely from their reading of my autobiography, which was the seed for this book. They were able to understand why I kept hiding my background, why I withheld information that I considered potentially hurtful to them. Our expanded communication engendered frank and honest dialogue and cleared up old misunderstandings. Such was frequently the case between parents and children for many of my witnesses.

My eldest daughter hoped that her children would live rich Jewish lives, and indeed they do. My younger daughter sent her son to a Jewish preschool, and he continues in kindergarten in a Jewish day school. In terms of passing the "torch" of communication about the Holocaust on to the next generation, I am confident that my grandchildren will do so once they build their own lives. Then they too will recover the "torch," will carry it transformed, and, as in Nadia's words, "The *Shoah* will never be forgotten."

ACKNOWLEDGEMENTS

My gratitude goes to Roy, my husband, for his constant support, his encouragement and his help. I am thankful to my daughter Michelle for her sound suggestions, her support, her many hours spent at the computer helping me in preparing the manuscript, and her careful reading of the work. I thank my daughter Claudette for her sustained encouragement.

I am grateful to Michal and Amnon Beit-Aharon for their hospitality at Kibbutz Alonim, and especially to Michal for locating the many witnesses for me for this project in Israel.

I thank Frederika Mandelbaum Shavit and Abraham Shavit for hosting us and advising us in Jerusalem.

I am very grateful to the people of The Hidden Child Foundation in New York for finding witnesses for me. This is also the case for L'Enfant Caché in Paris. I also thank my friends Rose Abendstern of Cambridge Massachusetts and of Paris, and Sylvie Kolton of Paris, as well as the many other friends in the United States and abroad who assisted me in this endeavor. I greatly appreciate the help of Myriam Frumer of Nivelles, Belgium, in obtaining the cooperation of the group of witnesses in Brussels, Belgium.

I extend my appreciation to the members of my writing group for their useful recommendations and constructive criticism of various chapters. I appreciate especially the comments of Marsha White, Laurie Noble, Lucille Cannava, and Elizabeth Coons.

My appreciation goes to George Brawerman for his artistic endeavor and for providing his photograph for the cover of this book.

I thank Eve Minkoff, my copy editor, for her careful work and her many suggestions.

Above all, I am deeply grateful to my witnesses—those featured in this book—as well as the many others whom I had the privilege of interviewing. I thank them for their openness. I am honored by their confidence in revealing their innermost personal thoughts and feelings. I was impressed by their intelligence and touched by their honesty.